smile
GUIDE

Employee
Perspectives
on Culture,
Loyalty, and Profit

smile
GUIDE

Employee
Perspectives
on Culture,
Loyalty, and Profit

PAUL SPIEGELMAN
Author of *Why Is Everyone Smiling?*

Brown Books Publishing Group
Dallas, Texas

Smile Guide
Employee Perspectives on Culture, Loyalty, and Profit

Brown Books Publishing Group
16250 Knoll Trail, Suite 205
Dallas, Texas 75248
www.BrownBooks.com
(972) 381-0009

ISBN 978-1-61254-038-2
Library of Congress Control Number: 2011942302

Printed in the United States of America
10 9 8 7 6 5 4 3 2 1

For more information, please visit www.SmileGuideBook.com

To all past, present, and future employees of
The Beryl Companies, this is your story.

Contents

Acknowledgments

In most books, the author is thanking everyone that supported the book process. In this case, I'm actually thanking the authors, the twenty-four Beryl employees who took the time and effort to lend their insight and passion to the *Smile Guide*. The concepts, execution, and results are due to their commitment to the company and their desire for other business leaders to learn the Beryl Way. I will forever be thankful for their contributions.

I also want to thank Craig Hanley, who had the job of putting up with all of our personalities while helping us put our thoughts into words.

I must also recognize my family—my mom and dad, who supported their sons starting a business together; my brother Mark, one of the company's cofounders; and my late brother, Barry, whose spirit lives on in our culture every day.

I feel fortunate to have been put in the position of trying to impact the lives of people who have worked with us. I would like to thank the readers in advance for embarking on a similar journey to discover that the best road to business success is within your own four walls.

Introduction

Four years ago, I wrote *Why Is Everyone Smiling?* The book challenged fellow business leaders to stop treating employees like commodities, and it hit a nerve. As flattered as I was by requests for media interviews and speaking engagements, the keen response confirmed my allegation that there's a pressing need for evolution in American corporate culture.

More than anything else, I was saddened to see the most commonsensical premises of the book regarded as revelations. Take pains to provide employees with a caring environment? Reach out to help them in times of need? As much as I enjoyed promoting the message, I also got a little frustrated when speaking to classes of students who couldn't begin to fathom the notion that a people-focused culture can make a huge difference on any company's road to success.

Why is a company with a positive culture such an exception these days? Why do so many new hires at Beryl feel compelled to tell me how special the company is—and how surprised they are to find a workplace that finally treats them like human beings? When I scour the business press looking for similar examples, what I tend to find is a superabundance of "come from behind" stories—companies hoping that high-risk strategies will pull them out of the very nonstrategic holes they dug. Rarely do I see profiles of highly profitable firms doing things the right way year in and year out—companies that have their basic ups and downs, but whose overall steady growth isn't hampered by these natural fluctuations.

It's only natural for the general media to focus on things that drag an economy down: a handful of big, foundering public companies and a rogues' gallery of CEOs. But it's a shame that American business has been getting such a bad rap. Well-run companies—typically unsung, privately held outfits—are the country's best hope for steady, long-term job growth. And we need to understand that people will be the real power of a revitalized economy, not a few trendy products or the troubled companies in the headlines. If compassionate, ethical enterprises become the rule instead of the exception, business will be much better positioned to create more sustainable employment and greater long-term growth.

Over the last twenty-five years Beryl has honed a dependable method for double-digit revenue growth, achieving five to six times the profitability of our competitors and holding a client retention rate of 96 percent. Overwhelmingly, we owe that success to a people-centric culture based on our Circle of Growth™ philosophy: employee loyalty driving customer satisfaction, which in turn drives profit.

Some might argue that while Beryl has a nice culture and a profitable business model, it is difficult to quantify the connection between people and profits. Indeed, many business leaders still believe that culture has no ROI. Yet there is mounting evidence that the best, most profitable companies happen to share Beryl's multi-stakeholder approach. In the 2007 book, *Firms of Endearment*, David Wolfe chronicles the experiences of a number of companies that put employees and customers in front of other stakeholders— companies like Whole Foods, Southwest Airlines, The Container Store, and Harley-Davidson, to name a few. In the ten-year period ending in June 2006, these companies returned 1,026 percent to their investors. During the same period, the companies chronicled in Jim Collins's book *Good to Great* returned 333 percent and the S&P 500 returned 122 percent.

Our core business is providing outsourced customer service solutions in the healthcare industry. We serve over five hundred hospitals throughout the US and have turned a commodity business (call centers) into a service for which our customers are willing to pay a premium price. We help improve the patient experience across the entire continuum of care, touching patients before, during, and after care. Our secret is to connect our culture to our customers and, in turn, be able to invest our profits back into our people to give them better resources to do their jobs.

This book is a road map for making that exceptional model the rule. It provides readers with a wealth of practical resources and ideas—culture tips and tools—that can be implemented immediately at little or no cost. Ultimately, the goal is to erase the false perception that business owners and senior managers must choose between sustained growth and evolving their culture. You can struggle to trim expenses and boost sales all you want, but building and maintaining a great culture is the ultimate road to stable economic rewards.

While no CEO is going to discount the role of a leader, in most companies results really are determined by other people. Truly great cultures tend to be bottom-up in nature, and the format of this book is a case in point. While the business world constantly hears from consultants, authors, and opinionated company founders, the real story of commerce is occasionally much better told by the women and men who live it day in and day out at multiple levels within a specific organization.

The text in your hands delivers real-world experience in the words of accomplished professionals who live their jobs very thoughtfully indeed. They speak for 350 Beryl coworkers who, having been given a purpose and the opportunity, are responsible for creating and sustaining the company. The power of everything—from our core values to our future vision—is theirs, and so is the right to tell the story. They haven't sugar-coated the many mistakes we've made along the way, and the chapter on challenges is a particularly up-front and insightful account of hard lessons learned.

As a CEO, it's fair for me to point out that the best bottom-up cultures get started when people at "the top" of an outmoded organization finally wake up to the connection between financial rewards and a positive, intimate culture. Recently I spoke to forty executives at a company in terrible shape. They had killer competitors and union problems, abysmal employee engagement, and—consequently—dangerously low customer satisfaction levels. When they asked how to turn the culture around, I told them to get ready to take a long and painfully honest look in the mirror.

I told them that they would have to publicly own up to the fact that their culture wasn't what they'd like it to be and admit to their employees that they saw a need for change. They would have to be inclusive and engage all the employees in shaping and executing the plan. And I warned them that this immensely fulfilling journey would probably take years. Neglected cultures breed mistrust, and you can't just pass out a list of upcoming events one morning and announce that you're implementing a shiny new ethos. No one would buy in to that facile approach.

Building a solid culture program is a long process and hard work, but you will find the tips and tools in this book a proven means of generating small impacts that can absolutely change your organization for the better over time. As your financials improve, you will achieve more satisfying business goals in the process: creating a great place to work, providing great customer service, and making great community contributions.

Start today!

—Paul Spiegelman

Evolving a Culture

By Lara Morrow

Lara has been with us for over ten years. Her full-time job is helping to enhance and protect our culture. She has an incredible ability to move from planning an important event to having a tough conversation with an employee who is taking advantage of the culture. She reports to me because she has her hand on the pulse of the organization and I want people to understand that culture is discussed at every leadership meeting we have. In the book she is referred to as the culture director, but her official title is queen of fun and laughter. She's going to tell you how to build a culture from the ground up—with little or no money.

—Paul

If the idea of rolling out a progressive culture-enhancement program in your organization intimidates you in any way, please rest easy. Culture evolution is a slow buy-in process, so every firm should start small and proceed at a comfortable pace. Beryl certainly started small and nonstrategically. When I came onboard as HR coordinator in 2000, the person responsible for the holiday parties let it be known that she was tired of arranging those festivities. Someone said, "Lara can do 'em," and without much premeditation I said, "OK."

Start Small

I'd never planned a corporate event, and when I was hired they handed me a social committee checkbook with a balance of $46.25. Before we could have any sort of celebration, we had to raise money first with a bake sale, a carwash, or a "Blue Jeans for Bucks Day." This promoted employee buy-in, and with fresh money in the account, we could then splurge for candy and cake at Halloween. When we designed more ambitious events, nobody complained. The contests and happenings gradually got bigger and more elaborate, and on randomly designated days, visitors to the facility would find the entire workforce wearing pajamas or crazy hats. We often did things we used to do in high school and had a blast doing it!

Essentially, we were simply paying tribute to the spirit of fun that the Spiegelman brothers had kept alive at Beryl since they founded the company. Their approach to business was primarily grounded in creating a sense of family with employees, but they were also young entrepreneurs who weren't afraid to add a bit of playfulness to day-to-day operations. They enjoyed roller hockey in the parking lot, practical jokes, and occasional demonstrations of goofiness that weren't stereotypical C-level behaviors.

Employees found the informality refreshing, and our growing program of events turned this fun orientation into a dominant component of the culture. We also noticed that the culture was generating an enthusiasm and loyalty that had a significant impact on employee performance, retention, and customer satisfaction.

Around 2003, we bumped up the culture budget to leverage the advantages further and it began attracting regular media attention. This eventually led us to winning many "best place to work" awards.

As the company grew, I couldn't keep up with both the culture program and my primary role in HR. Motivating 350 coworkers was easier for me than managing three, and I relished the creative aspects of my duties a lot more than administering 401(k) plans. A peer who believed that culture should become a separate department suggested I move my interests in that direction. He said that culture was our sustainable advantage and we should have someone dedicated to it permanently. The move was also in line with the company's custom of putting people in positions that best utilize their strengths.

Fun?

After some discussions with Paul, I took charge of the program full-time. Well before this, I'd acquired the nickname "Queen of Fun and Laughter," and this ended up sticking. We also eventually designated our new head of HR the vice president of the Department of Great People and Fun. The word "fun" can sound trivial—even ludicrous—in a business context, but we have the metrics to prove that the concept has serious strategic and financial value. Fun is not by any means the only anchor of our culture, which is formally grounded in service, quality, ethics, and camaraderie. We're equally committed to transparency, approachability, and other noble corporate virtues explained in the chapters that follow. As the queen of fun and laughter, however, I don't mind explaining the value of fun and the point of parties like our annual Family Day celebration.

On a convenient Saturday every spring, we transform our parking lot into a free four-hour carnival for employees and their families. Diversions at Family Day include bounce houses, inflatable slides, bungee trampolines, ponies, a petting zoo, obstacle courses, face painting, games, and tons of food. Employees are supposed to bring only their immediate family members; single employees can bring a friend or nieces and nephews. Every year at least one employee will bring every person on their block, a transgression our chief operating officer shrugs off philosophically. There can often be a challenge in keeping these events limited to coworkers and a few guests. Coworkers sometimes "extend" their immediate family members in order to bring more to the fun events. Although it is a huge compliment to us that others outside the company want to attend, we simply don't have the bandwidth to open them up to the public. So to remain in control of attendance, we have conversations as necessary with individuals who take advantage of the events.

As the years have passed, we've learned that the spirit generated by events like Family Day and our Fourth of July cookouts has a powerful and enduring life of its own. It costs next to nothing to grill hot dogs and arrange the potluck sides, but employees find invaluable joy in dunking their CEO in a dunk tank and drenching one another in water balloon and water gun fights.

They love our Gong Show, too, where senior leaders will judge twenty-plus acts and hand out awards for Most Embarrassing Performance and Most Painful Performance to Watch—as well as spontaneous kudos like this year's awards for Sexiest Janet Jackson Lookalike and Best Blind Soul Singer. Our recent Amazing Race competition is an example of how a progressive culture can tie fun directly to critical business initiatives.

Sometimes fun is the sole purpose of the festive approach that makes us unique in our very competitive industry—an industry we dominate because our coworkers consistently demonstrate great focus and intensity. On other occasions, the fun is just the most visible element of an employee engagement strategy that is always geared toward fostering loyalty and productivity.

Embedding a Bottom-Up Approach

As our business grew, it became clear that the culture could never fully take root if it was charted and controlled by a small group of senior executives. It had to be owned by each individual in the organization. With no particularly clear vision, I recruited several of the key "drivers of the spirit" in the company. The first meeting was six people staring at one another in my office, unsure of what to discuss. We jotted down the company's traditional annual events and discussed the pros and cons of each. Great ideas emerged in subsequent monthly meetings, and as we began to see improvements add up we formally christened the group the Better Beryl Bureau—BBB for short.

Initially the sole purpose of this embryonic culture committee was to plan and man parties. They would decorate, shop for food, make game booths, stuff treat bags, deliver invitations, and paint signs. They arrived early to set up, left late after cleaning up, and sacrificed their own relaxation time to create fun for coworkers. New members were inducted twice a year. These had to be dependable high-performers and natural leaders. Today, every applicant writes an open letter explaining why they want to join, with recommendation letters from one peer and one manager. These applicants are interviewed and selected by current members.

As the committee grew, there was always much to discuss and never enough time. Some members were noticeably passionate about one aspect of the culture and indifferent to all others, so we divided the group into subcommittees:

- Events
- Recognition and Morale
- Internal Communication
- Outreach
- Onboarding
- Caring

These six themes tended to stand out in every meeting and seemed to be the defining contours of our culture. (Every organization is going to have different emphases depending on who they are and what they do.)

The key idea here is maximizing employee involvement to achieve a critical mass of positive influencers. Each subcommittee has ten to fifteen members. The commitment for a subcommittee leader is one year, but if it's not working out on either side we can make a change at any time. If the leaders are successful, they can continue in their role. The leaders tend to be original BBB members with great initiative and heart. They set the agendas for their own meetings and send out minutes afterward, putting in at least five extra hours a week while the general member averages one hour.

I mentor the leaders on challenges and we have regular one-on-one meetings where I walk them through everything they need to do. We give them autonomy to develop their own ideas and a ton of visibility that helps their career paths. This leadership development component has become a great "farm team" for the company.

The contributions of the different subcommittees are cited throughout the book, but the following synopsis of the Recognition and Morale team gives a more thorough idea of how profoundly the Better Beryl Bureau has embedded itself in the environment it continues to serve and shape. The power of our bottom-up approach to culture could not be better illustrated.

Fifty Extra Sets of Antennae

Before the advent of the BBB, we assumed that we were recognizing all high-performing individuals for their efforts. We also assumed that the company's open-door policy gave everyone a chance to communicate issues affecting morale. Wrong on both counts! It turns out we had many unsung heroes and quite a few recent hires who didn't trust our promise of immunity for free speech. With a subcommittee dedicated to recognition and morale, things slowly but surely began to change for the better.

The doubters began to use the Recognition and Morale team as a safe conduit of information and a mechanism to funnel their grievances to management. The team members also worked side by side with humble individuals who shined in their jobs but never self-promoted. With twenty new sets of antennae scattered around the call center, management was suddenly much more connected to the heart of the hive. Rumors and morale issues could be identified and addressed in real time, and we were finally able to recognize quiet contributors who had previously been underappreciated. The entire Better Beryl Bureau has about fifty members from every level of the organization, so that's effectively fifty sets of antennae—or fifty sets of feet on the street—with the company's best interests at heart.

Coaching was required to fine-tune this unique early warning system, and I tried to teach the subcommittee members how to detect trends in coworker remarks that might merit the attention of senior leadership. When they do bring urgent feedback, we pay very close attention. A new senior vice president was let go after our R&M antennae detected her remarkably negative effect on morale. When the team let us know their coworkers "absolutely hated" a revised attendance policy, we were also able to address that situation proactively.

The R&M team is not seen as management's spies. They're all well-respected as individuals, and they know the difference between promoting transparency and being snitches. But if they do run across an issue that could jeopardize an aspect of the organization, they know they have an obligation to relay the information. If I agree, I'll say, "You're right, we really need to go talk to the COO about this." And I'll take them with me and let them have the experience of communicating a serious morale issue to a senior officer. The chief operating officer regularly sits in on the last fifteen minutes of both the R&M subcommittee and the Communications subcommittee. It's these two forums where the most urgent nitty-gritty issues usually pop up.

It's important that your culture committee members feel totally safe and comfortable telling senior management *anything* that's on their minds. It's also important not to treat them exclusively like one-way conduits of information. When appropriate, I teach them how to go back and respond to complaints in a way that saves management the unnecessary step: "This isn't a big deal and here's why. Go back and talk to the person and tell them this." Eventually they learn to handle situations on their own, and it's a great way to incubate new leaders.

Having a team of trusted ear-to-the-ground people who know what's going on is invaluable. We all know that a core factor in every organization is how individuals feel about the way they are treated, respected, and valued for what they do. Morale, turnover, and hiring and training costs revolve around this fact. But seriously, who has time to monitor the mood swings of every trouper every day? And how valuable would it be to your organization to have a volunteer team constantly focused on questions like, "Are we neglecting a certain group or individual?" "Is there anybody who worked on a project that needs special recognition?"

The main task of the twenty R&M team members is to keep morale high by making sure *everybody* feels recognized. They help me plan events that acknowledge departments, groups, or individuals who have worked especially hard on a project. If the IT department is burned out, it's the R&M team that comes together and arranges to send them offsite for some rest and relaxation. They recently orchestrated a surprise "Nerd Day" for IT. We catered a lunch, put up pictures of popular Hollywood nerd characters, and the entire company dressed as nerds. Our tech team was surprised and thought the whole thing was hysterical.

If one of our patient-experience advocate groups is getting a ton of unexpected call volume because the hospital or physician's office client sent out a mailer and forgot to tell us about it, the R&M team comes to me and says, "Hey, these folks are getting slammed and attitudes are way down; is there anything we can do for them?" If I agree, the R&M team brings in muffins, fruit, and juice the next morning and caters to the beleaguered group. They feel comfortable getting senior leadership involved, and they recently planned for the CEO and COO to pass out ice cream to everyone while dressed as old-fashioned ice cream shop attendants!

If the R&M team leader learns that understaffing is an issue in this case, she'll take it upon herself to go ask HR when the next class of trainees will be ready to help. Then she'll relay that info to her leader on the Communications subcommittee, who will add the good news to her weekly company-wide e-mail: "Great news! A new trainee class starts Monday! Hang in there, guys! Help is on the way!" This kind of spontaneous internal messaging from peers can be much more welcome at times than management's perspective.

The Missing Link

The idea of a fully empowered, focused, and wide-ranging employee culture committee is a transformative idea. Our Better Beryl Bureau has enabled us to capture and direct critical organizational mass that we were missing previously. It's just wrongheaded for a senior management team to stand up and say, "Listen up! This is the way it's going to be around here!" A culture program needs the weight of the whole company, and once you have the critical mass it starts happening on its own. The fifty-plus people currently on the BBB represent roughly one-sixth of all employees, and it took a few years for them to coalesce.

That ratio seems to be ideal for us because this peer group of mostly hourly employees now drives the whole culture program effectively—from the bottom up. All I do is monitor a few meetings, mentor, and try to determine exactly how much formal responsibility these ambassadors can handle without interfering with their daily job responsibilities or duties better left to management. To date, we've found them remarkably capable, but if you don't pick the right people it won't work. Culture committee members—especially the leaders—have to be mature and have a lot of common sense, which sadly isn't always an easy combination to find. Regularly recognizing the achievements of members has helped us recruit applicants. The first thing new hires immediately want to know is, "How can I get on the Better Beryl Bureau?"

The Ultimate Virtue—Patience

You have to make culture's critical importance visible to everyone. I report directly to Paul because the person responsible for culture has to be able to point to anybody—or any process or action—in the organization and say, "We're not living up to our values *here*," or "We have a serious problem *here*." The chief operating officer manages me on a day-to-day basis because I have a million ideas and somebody has to filter them. My primary role is making sure the company stays true to its core values as we grow. The queen of fun and laughter is the keeper of the flame, and she makes sure we're doing things the "Beryl Way"!

Our culture has evolved tremendously in the last decade and there's no doubt that our penchant for fun has contributed mightily to our success along the way. My closing advice to business owners and managers who are serious about culture: you can still get started with a budget of $46.25! So many of our original efforts were shoestring affairs, and there's real value in the make-do creativity required to pull them off. Before we built the structure into our program, we built a lot of great teams—and memories—just by sitting down together and cutting and pasting paper decorations.

Tips and Tools

1. **Be prepared to evolve your culture slowly.**
   - A vibrant culture can take years to establish.
   - Start small: experiment with a single department.
   - A serious commitment from top management is mandatory.

2. **Define your culture before you put the program in action.**
   - What are the philosophies that you live by?
   - Ask employees to identify four ideal core values.
   - If "fun" isn't part of your approach, what is?
   - What other words describe your culture? Respect? Loyalty? Openness?

3. **Empower the person in charge of the culture program. He or she . . .**
   - . . . should report directly to—and be respected by—the president or CEO.
   - . . . should be responsible for the company's adherence to core values.
   - . . . should be responsible for the employee culture committee.
   - . . . must be free of bias and able to look at situations and people nonjudgmentally.
   - . . . must be able to stand up for employees and disagree with senior leadership on decisions.

4. Event planning can be a logical place to start.
   - Put together a realistic calendar of events.
   - Recruit a planning and execution committee.
   - Be frank with members about time commitments and responsibilities.
   - Reward active participants with recognition.
   - Ask employees what they would enjoy.
   - Hold simple fundraisers to help with budgeting.

5. Consider an employee culture committee as an ultimate program goal.
   - Be selective and require applicants to have manager approval.
   - Establish subcommittees based on pressing needs.
   - Mentor subcommittee leaders in regular meetings.
   - Define a target ratio of committee membership to workforce. One to six? One to twenty?
   - Have a senior leader manage the committee.

2

Recruiting and Talent

By Glenda Dearion, Andrew Pryor, and Maricela Rodriguez

If you do nothing else, you need to revisit how you hire people. We are always in a rush to hire, but we don't always realize the tremendous risk we are taking. How do we know we are hiring the right people? By first hiring people who know how to hire the right people. Glenda is a master recruiter. I don't know how many times people have told me how Glenda "sold" them on Beryl. Maricela has been part of our operations team for fifteen years and knows how to recognize empathy and compassion like no other. Andrew leads our HR team and doesn't sacrifice the discipline needed to put someone through multiple interviews or behavioral scenarios. You'll learn in this chapter about how to measure fit as well as skill, and the relative importance of each.

—Paul

People tend to be the heart and soul of any enterprise, and Beryl is certainly no exception to the rule. Clients basically trust our employees to be their face and voice in the world, and we have developed manpower strategies and hiring tactics that help us keep that trust intact. While this chapter describes the procedures with some details that are specific to our industry, the guiding principles and approach are easily adaptable to other environments.

Right Skills, Right Fit

Every job applicant goes through a slow and well-planned hiring process. Ultimately, talent has to fit a specific role, so we focus on the exact competencies required for success in each position long before we start interviewing. Knowing that applicants who end up in the wrong role will never live up to their full potential, we work hard to make sure we select people who both fit the culture and have skills that are an excellent match for the job we need them to do. To determine the necessary skill sets, we analyze what makes our best coworkers successful in light of our current strategic objectives.

Small, high-performance companies move quickly and need people who can fit in with the dynamics of the culture and business environment. We like to say that only 49 percent of a person's success in this kind of environment will be determined by his or her technical skills. Fifty-one percent comes from the ability to fit into the culture, build peer relationships, and manage upward. At the average company, the ratio is probably 80 percent skills, 20 percent fit. When we hire, we're always looking for our ideal 49:51 ratio. This applies to everyone—patient-experience advocates, accountants, administrative assistants, and executives. No matter how good you are technically, you won't last here if you can't fit in.

Attracting Candidates

Our culture program has proved an invaluable recruiting asset. We want culture to be a major factor in the applicant's decision to join the "family," so we promote it heavily on our website, www.Beryl. net. Instead of the usual formal headshots, the bios of key personnel show photos of the individuals competing in a fencing contest or riding the log flume with her family at SeaWorld. Applicants who visit the website also see our famous inverted pyramid:

Coworkers at the top, senior leaders at the bottom! In a very real sense, this concept is more important than our logo. It's the honest reality of who we are. And the idea of employees being at the top of your pyramid and driving your culture is absolutely exportable.

Because we're so employee-focused, Beryl has repeatedly been named one of the best places to work, including being ranked the No. 2 Best Medium-Sized Company to Work for in America. We mention this on the website and in corporate materials, and it's prominently noted in the lobby. When candidates are searching our website or when they come in to interview, they're wondering, "What makes this place so special?" Once they understand that the awards are given as a result of employee surveys, it makes us even more attractive.

> *When candidates are in my office, so many tell me, "This place feels really welcoming." From the minute they walk into the lobby to the minute they walk out, they notice that everyone has a smile on their face. Employees are talking to one another, and they tend to spontaneously include visitors in those conversations. This isn't anything that we plan or tell our employees to do. The funniest part is when candidates ask me, "Why is everyone smiling?" They have no idea that our CEO wrote a book called* Why Is Everyone Smiling? *So I have fun asking them to turn around and look at the copy of the book displayed in my office. That always starts a good chuckle.*
>
> *—Glenda*

Thanks to our reputation as an innovative employer, our executives are frequently asked to speak at colleges, which provides great local visibility and is a big plus for recruiting. MBA professors at Southern Methodist University, Texas Christian University, and the local University of Texas campus invite us to coach their students on how to do an ROI on a culture that treats people right. When higher-education institutions like these tour their brightest scholarship students through our facility so that we can explain the Beryl Way to them, it's invaluable exposure for everyone. Every time we give those speeches, a handful of students apply to work here—good, strong candidates who just happened to be in the audience. Even more valuable than explaining the Beryl Way is allowing the students or candidates to see a progressive culture in action.

If job candidates happen to show up on Pajama Day or Crazy Hat Day, we hear a lot of, "Wow!" Last Halloween, the whole operations management team was dressed up in sixties- and seventies-era attire while we did interviews. We sat there decked out like flower children, and the candidates kept saying, "Man, you guys really have a *good time* at work!" It's an effective way of demonstrating that this kind of participation is a crucial part of the job. Applicants have called back and asked, "Should I show up in pajamas for my second interview? Should I wear a funny hat?" Our current training manager showed up for his December interview in an unusually loud Hawaiian shirt featuring images of Santa Claus. It was a good indication that he knew what he was jumping into!

Our referral program attracts a ton of candidates. In fact, more than 50 percent of new hires come from employees referring friends and family members—undeniable proof of the culture's appeal. Occasionally, it's embarrassing for a referring employee if a family member or friend doesn't make the cut. We never bring it up, but sometimes you'll hear a person say, "My cousin would have been great here, but she didn't pass the assessments." But every coworker understands that the hiring process is stringent, and most employees won't recommend someone who wouldn't make them proud.

We always treat candidates with the dignity and respect we would want. Every person who walks through the door continues to tell the Beryl story whether or not we hire them. One lady in a recent new-hire class said she'd heard about the company from a friend who interviewed but didn't get the job. Her friend told her she'd been treated so well as a job candidate she knew Beryl would be an awesome place to work.

People attracted to the culture have gone to great—and sometimes outrageous—lengths to get a foot in the door. In his previous book, Paul mentions that we frequently send gift baskets to current and prospective clients, so one savvy job-seeker sent him a gorgeous basket with a brilliant letter full of references to ideas in the book. This earned her big points for creativity, and we gave her a shot.

The most extreme example of the culture's drawing power is probably the woman who wanted to work here so badly that she kept applying under different names. Each time she was declined, she'd adopt an alias and try to sneak back into the interview process. This went on half a dozen times. We laugh about it now, but we're proud of it, too.

Recently a new hire ran up to one of our administrative assistants. He was all excited and said, "Hey, I made it!" She gave him a friendly but uncertain smile and welcomed him to the company, and he said, "You don't remember me, but I'm Mike, the Subway delivery man. I've been bringing catered lunches here for years, and I've also been applying here the whole time. Now I've finally got a job at Beryl! Isn't it great?"

—Glenda

A Slow Process

The lengthy, deliberate recruiting process starts with our talent-acquisition team screening all résumés. For exempt-level positions, the team forwards approved résumés to the appropriate manager. For nonexempt positions like patient-experience advocates (the employees in our call center), our recruiter reviews the résumés for people with solid customer service backgrounds, tenure in previous positions, and demonstrated critical-thinking skills.

Candidates for exempt-level senior positions typically visit our campus at least three times and will interact with as many as eight to ten coworkers during the process. Candidates may go through at least seven interviews; one had eighteen interviews in a three-month period.

We want to see a different aspect of the candidate in every interview, so there's a breakfast setting, a lunch, and a dinner. People loosen up when food is involved or when there's a casual conversation going on, and we scrutinize every interaction. If the candidate is rude or dismissive to the waiter or to coworkers they meet during the process, they're probably not a good fit for the organization.

Another benefit of hiring slowly is that new hires feel comfortable on their first day at work. They know the facility, and they know they have the support of all the people who interviewed them.

> *A candidate was in our reception lobby waiting for an interview. After he was escorted to meet with the hiring manager, our director of first impressions (receptionist) told me that he was short with her and had a scowl on his face until the hiring manager came out to get him. All of a sudden, the smile was turned on. Needless to say, we didn't hire him.*
>
> *—Andrew*

Behavior-Based Interviewing

After many years of working in staffing and human resources, we've learned one firm and inescapable truth that we take pains to teach our hiring managers: it's all downhill from the interview! Think about it. Everyone has an interview suit, and everyone knows that they need to show up with shined shoes and clean fingernails, smiling and speaking as articulately as they possibly can. They will never look better or sound brighter, and from that moment on, frankly, it's simply *remarkable* how far and furiously downhill things can tumble. So we're big fans of behavior-based interviewing, which views past behavior as the best indicator of future performance. We ask very specific questions about things a candidate has done in the past to help us gauge how they might behave once hired.

We seek broad consensus on hires. After our new chief information officer had interviewed with the Strategic Leadership Team and two IT managers, we sat him down with four coworkers from the IT team. He said this final grilling was the toughest, but after he answered their questions the technicians unanimously said, "We can work with this guy." No one had veto power, but if anyone had expressed serious reservations we would have revisited the issue.

By involving those last four employees, we made them instant champions for the new CIO. They immediately went back to their teams and talked up his résumé and qualifications. And because they had skin in the game on this hire, they were going to do whatever they could to help him succeed.

> *When we hired our VP of operations, the candidates went through the culture interview and the usual interviews with supervisors and managers. We then specifically scheduled a lunch so a select group of our advocates—the call-takers who actually work the phones—could evaluate and give their input on the person who would control their work environment. And we paid very close attention to their feedback before we made an offer. That's a great example of how our bottom-up structure functions on a day-to-day basis.*
>
> *—Maricela*

Playing a Supporting Role

Managers at Beryl see themselves as "support staff" working to make sure the patient-experience advocates have everything they need to handle calls perfectly. Support staff must be able to talk freely to people in other departments, get feedback, and put a team together. Our managers are expected to fit in well enough to work the structure and advance needed changes. They can present change in ways that make their own managers say, "I trust this individual enough to back the initiative."

When people fail in support-staff roles, they typically weren't able to build critical internal relationships. They couldn't interact well enough with finance, for example, to make sure that funds were available for their ideas, or they weren't sufficiently connected to marketing and project management to realize that their change would adversely impact a new product. The most skilled programmer in the world will watch his ideas crash and burn here if he can't get out in front of folks and win their support. A skilled IT professional who can sell concepts, on the other hand, has the ability to gain buy-in and support. She'll be able to create a groundswell around her ideas, push them through internally, and improve the company in the process.

We hire people who buy in to our culture, people who want to participate. If you've hired for that, people are already open to anything and will jump into anything—recreational and operational. Folks who are saying, "I don't want to do that," aren't interacting and aren't building relationships. And no matter how technically or intellectually gifted they may be, they're not lasting because they can't get over their egos.

—Andrew

Check Your Ego at the Door

Because leaders need an especially healthy balance of fit and skills, we put all management candidates through an hour-long culture interview. The questions dig really deep and are exclusively designed to assess the person as a culture fit. Our culture director and an HR executive ask every candidate to talk about things that reveal personality. Tell us about something fun you did at your last job. What makes you laugh? What do you do to de-stress? The culture interview is one of our best tools. If people don't give us good answers, we know they're not good culture fits.

> *I always ask executive candidates, "You know, we have Pajama Day every week in December. Are you willing to wear pajamas to work?" Last year a candidate got huffy and said, "Absolutely not!" A week later, a recruiter friend of mine who facilitates a networking group told me that one of his members stood up and said, "You won't believe this, but an HR exec just asked me if I would wear pajamas to work. What does that have to do with my skills?" When my friend told me this story, I said, "Great! That's what the question is for. If he wasn't willing to wear pajamas, he wasn't going to fit in or be successful here." The interview did exactly what it was supposed to do.*
>
> *—Andrew*

We understand why a logical, task-oriented professional may not want to dress up and act crazy. From a strictly operational perspective, however, we also know that the intensity of our operation demands leaders who can *interact* enthusiastically with everybody. This openness to interaction is what we call supporting the culture.

On Crazy Hat Day, for example, it's a given that all patient-experience advocates are going to wear crazy hats. Are managers going to show some solidarity by joining in? Why not? Are they going to lead by example and support the patient-experience advocates on Family Day by grilling hot dogs and hamburgers for four hours when it's 105 degrees outside? That kind of servant leadership is a definite expectation.

No matter how silly the games and events may seem, you join in because you want to support the culture. Our chief operating officer has gone to great lengths to liven up several events and prove that he doesn't consider himself a god among men. You wouldn't expect to find a highly skilled strategist riding a Segway through a call center at high speeds in a coconut bra and a Mardi Gras wig made out of scarlet feathers, but that is precisely what you get here.

There is a healthy humility in this kind of goofiness that status-obsessed managers cannot come to grips with. They could never take a pie in the face or wash a direct report's car when that employee wins a contest. They worry that any act of humility on their part will undermine their aura of authority. Successful candidates don't have these hang-ups. Their attitude is, "Whatever you want me to do to support the culture, I'm going to do it." Crazy hats and pajamas are a lot of fun in their own right, but they also represent managerial talent liberated from ego and delusions of grandeur. Humbling yourself is a prerequisite for real leadership. It earns you respect that is ultimately more effective than raw authority.

Testing and Screening Our Leaders

Exempt-level employees go through personality testing, and we take those tests very seriously in the hiring process. We send a personality assessment test to the homes of candidates who make the final round. The questions help us get to know the management candidates better and assess their true fit and compatibility with the current team. We use the scores to compare the candidate to other people in the department, coworkers in the same positions, and the manager. It's a solid balance check, and scores that indicate a serious lack of balance may disqualify a candidate.

Tests also ensure honesty, because you're never sure if candidates are being truthful or just trying to tell you what you want to hear. If a score sends up a red flag, we either decline the person or dig a little deeper in a follow-up interview. Recently someone gave phenomenal interview answers, but the test showed him as weak—*way* too much into making other people happy. That's a concern, obviously, since we can't have a manager letting people take his kindness for weakness. This candidate knew that compassion is our top priority, and we suspected he was deliberately trying to give compassionate answers to every question. When we challenged him with tougher live interview questions, he gave good specific answers and passed. If tests show that a person has no compassion whatsoever, we decline automatically.

Hiring for Our Core Business

Preemployment assessments for nonexempt positions are also quite rigorous, but low turnover rates more than justify the long process. Most call centers never disclose their turnover rates, but the industry average is well over 100 percent. Our goal has always been the low 20 percent range and we manage to stay close to that. The following overview of our screening and hiring principles offers a model that can generate a similar competitive advantage for almost any business.

All candidates must have held a job for at least one year in the last three consecutive years. This one qualification eliminates the job-hoppers who typically account for 30 percent of applicants. Next, an initial behavior-based phone screening serves as a "get to know us" session where the talent manager talks a lot about Beryl. We want patient-experience advocates with critical thinking skills, people who can determine the needs of our clients' customers and maneuver through multiple computer screens while continuing to provide exceptional service to the person on the other end of the line. The talent manager also looks for personality and the kind of maturity that's essential for customer service workers who have to deal with the full spectrum of humanity—the good, the bad, and the ugly.

During this phone screening, we look for appealing voice tone and the all-important quality of compassion. We can teach people phone etiquette and how to navigate our software, but we can't teach them how to be compassionate to a caller who has just been diagnosed with cancer. Even callers who just need to find a new doctor tend to be a little anxious and stressed. If one of our advocates were to use slang or treat that caller abruptly, what kind of brand impression would that make on our client's behalf?

During the first interview, we actually ask every applicant to define "compassion." Essentially, the word means "helping, serving, and supporting others," but a lot of people put parameters around it. They'll say it's "helping, serving, and supporting others *who are less fortunate than I am.*" Or "helping, serving, and supporting others *one time.*" Or even "helping, serving, and supporting others *in order to help myself.*" This simple question weeds out another 30 percent of advocate applicants and a much greater portion of executive candidates. In a recent search for a technology vice president, 40 percent of the applicants couldn't properly define compassion.

Patient-experience advocate candidates who pass the first phone screening get invited to our facility for a three- to four-hour series of assessments and interviews. We test for spelling, listening, keyboarding, data entry, and other computer skills. Applicants put headphones on and listen to a call with lots of background noises—a doorbell ringing, kids crying, a dog barking. They have to pull data out of that call and enter it into a database. If they score 80 percent or higher on the spelling and listening tests and meet or exceed our keystroke requirement, they advance to an interview with our team leads, who ask behavior-based questions and listen for diction and voice tone.

If this goes well, we ask the candidates to sit side by side with a current patient-experience advocate and listen in on live calls. This exercise is a super-realistic job preview, and after half an hour or so a few applicants have said, "You know, I thought I wanted to work in a call center, but I probably couldn't sit here and do this all day." Typically, however, they're quizzing the advocates between calls. "Is this really a cool place to work? What do you like about working here?" Our people are very positive, so the candidates end up getting jazzed about Beryl.

During the final interview, our hiring managers may ask promising prospective hires to read a script and talk. By now, the applicant has relaxed a bit, which makes it easier for us to pick up on things like poor pronunciation and diction, slang, and grammatical errors. Our employees simply can't have flaws in these areas. Occasionally we find compassionate applicants who pass our assessments but still struggle with a regional dialect or accent. In those circumstances, we may send the applicant home and schedule a final phone screening with our operations managers for the next day. We remind the applicant before they leave that the purpose of the call is to see if they can speak in an accent-neutral voice tone. Sometimes they take that to heart and we're able to hire them; sometimes, no matter how much we love them, they can't overcome their accent.

We run thorough background screenings—criminal and educational—for all new hires. Our advocates regularly obtain confidential information when they handle calls, so we can't hire anyone with felonies on their records. We also do a standard ten-panel drug test. The hiring manager has explained these requirements carefully up front, so we don't have to decline too many candidates who receive offers.

> *From a nonexempt perspective, naturally we want to hire people who are reliable and committed, so we have a very strict attendance policy. We ask two questions: "What do you consider good attendance?" and "If we called your previous manager, what would they say about your attendance?" The attendance message is a crucial part of the hiring process; it's preached incessantly from the start and new hires sign a form indicating that they understand the policy.*
>
> *—Maricela*

Orientation and the Buddy System

Orientation for nonexempt new hires is an enjoyable and memorable celebration. We gather them in the lobby and walk them into a training room full of balloons. They're greeted by multitudes of current employees—managers and patient-experience advocates—who are all clapping and cheering and dancing to loud music. We love to play the Sister Sledge song "We Are Family" because we always treat employees as an integral part of the Beryl family. We go around the room and the employees introduce themselves to the new hires. We tell them who we are, give a little description of our individual roles, and share some personal experiences at Beryl. It's a really warm introduction that lasts about half an hour.

Once the welcoming group leaves the room, our culture director and vice president of HR begin the orientation process by stressing three things:

- **"My job matters!"** We want new hires to know that the work they do for our company is vitally important *to other human beings*. They *matter* to the callers whom they will connect to qualified physicians. The connection they make for that person may very well help save his or her life! This focus on the positive social end results of the work an employee contributes is a tremendously powerful motivational tool.

- **"I'm going places!"** From day one, we emphasize the career runway and advancement opportunities the company provides so that every employee can build better lives for themselves and their families.

- **"I'm special!"** Finally, we explain our hiring strategy and the fact that their profiles indicate they have a unique competency for compassion. We tell them, "You can go home today and let your family members and significant others know that you're a genuinely compassionate person. We know that for a fact because we've screened you for compassion throughout this entire process."

Throughout the new hires' first day, we make sure they get the official scoop on the company: who we are, what we do, what we like, and the basic rules. An HR rep reviews policies, procedures, and benefits, and senior leaders come in one by one during these presentations to give brief overviews of their departments. Everyone tells a success story—or a "not so successful" story—to help break the ice and to familiarize new hires with the Beryl Way. Finally, we break bread together during a lunch provided by the company—a natural family gesture. During lunch, we play holiday videos from previous years. This allows new hires to get a feel for what the Beryl family is all about. When lunch is over, we have the new hires go on a scavenger hunt. We split them up into teams and provide them with the first clue. Then they move through the building hunting for answers (we make sure they stop at important departments to help them learn more about Beryl). Everyone who participates in the scavenger hunt receives a goody bag that contains branded items such as stress balls, a pen, a small notebook, and a slinky. These items are helpful when trying to stay focused during the two-week training program. The team that completes the scavenger hunt first wins gift cards to a local restaurant.

The Beryl Buddies program is a phenomenal culture tool that goes hand in hand with orientation. Our employee culture committee—the BBB—has an orientation team that assigns a buddy to each new hire. The buddies are there for mental and emotional support, to encourage the new hires, and to keep the warm feeling from orientation alive.

A buddy gives his or her new hire a more extensive introduction to the facility: where all the different departments are located and who works where. Our culture director keeps a supply of pens, memo pads, calendars, and other gifts the buddies can use to put goody bags together. They leave encouraging notes on their new hire's desk: "Can I help you with anything?" "Keep up the good work!" "Do you want to go to lunch?" Messages like these are extremely reassuring to a person going through the normal stress of a new job.

Buddies are all successful employees, so new hires can consult them on technical questions and performance issues. Your buddy is someone you can go to and say, "Hey, I'm having a hard time closing calls. If a caller is really chatty, what can I say to get them off the phone politely? What has worked for you?"

And buddies can level with new hires in a nonthreatening way: "Hey, Beth, you're doing awesome, but yesterday I heard you use the phrase, 'I'm *fixin' to* search for that information.' Try to say something like, '*Please let me* search for that information.'" We keep the buddy system in action throughout an employee's training, which can vary from two to five weeks.

All the buddies are volunteers, and they genuinely enjoy the experience. We never have to hunt down people and coerce them into being buddies. It's a "Let me! Let me!" situation. A lot of the buddies are managers who have mentored many different new hires.

—Maricela

Tips and Tools

1. **Use the power of your culture as a recruiting asset.**
   - Your website and collateral materials should make it clear that employees are the top priority in your culture.
   - Proudly display ways that your company has been recognized. Share your awards . . . or serious aspirations to win some.
   - Do you give existing employees a chance to share the story through a referral program?
   - Do you have a key iconic element that tells your "inverted pyramid" story?
   - During interviews, do you explain unique programs to job candidates?
   - Do your customers know how intensely and creatively you empower and nurture your troops—for *their* benefit?
   - What benefits could your firm realize from better promotion of your:
     a. Dress code?
     b. Community speaking engagements?
     c. "Best place to work" awards?

2. **Focus on the key competencies.**
   - Do you know the key competencies needed for success in your company and in the role you are hiring for? If not, define them!
   - Screen applicants against those competencies throughout the entire hiring process.

3. **Emphasize "Right Skills, Right Fit" over skills alone—especially with leaders.**
   - Use specific culture interviews to dig deep into your organization's identified key competencies:

33

a. Personalities
b. Openness to interaction
c. Capacity for servant leadership
d. Humility necessary for true leadership
- Focus on relationship-building skills and the ability to work the structure and advance change.

4. **Take time to find the right person based on the identified competencies.**
   - Put all candidates through multiple interviews.
   - Identify required competencies and design interviews to test for those competencies.
   - Seek and build internal consensus on hires.
   - Employ rigorous testing and screenings.
   - Provide an opportunity for a realistic job preview.

5. **Make a great first impression.**
   - Formalize an orientation process.
   - Start with an uplifting welcoming ceremony.
   - Experiment with a buddy program to help new hires get plugged into the system early.

3

Learning and Growth

By Bob Willey, Jhan Knebel, and Jennifer McDonald

Training gets a bad rap. In fact, in many companies when times get tough, training is the first to go. For small companies, it is especially difficult to have a "learning environment." They just don't have the resources. The result is that they're really not giving their employees the growth opportunities they deserve. Not so at Beryl. Our budget for training grows every year. In this chapter, you'll hear from Jennifer, whose infectious enthusiasm envelops every new class of patient-experience advocates. Jhan is a dedicated curriculum developer, ensuring that we can teach what we preach. Bob focuses on leadership training, making sure that we are identifying and mentoring our next generation of managers.

—Paul

Our Center for Learning and Growth—what other companies would call a training department—provides a variety of services that help the organization improve performance across the board. A good mirror of the company, the team is an entrepreneurial mix of tradition and innovation. We preserve key values and cultural components while the company grows, and we develop new support programs like leadership training and introductions to new clients and systems. Team members are lifelong learners, solidly supported by an organization that's big on personal improvement.

The team is constantly assessing what we're doing and how we can do it better. Is a program still relevant just because we've been doing it for eight years? What tweaks does the curriculum need? Trainers study the specific changing demands of all jobs to see whether we're still meeting needs and where fresh ideas are required. The energy and enthusiasm that we bring to training has an impact.

We have solid executive team-building and situational training programs and a mandatory introductory training program for all exempt hires called the Beryl Way. In addition, all exempt new hires who are responsible for helping our clients understand our core business are required to attend patient-experience advocate training. We think it's critical for them to be intimately familiar with the day-to-day rigors of taking calls before they take on the responsibility of advising our clients. Unlike a lot of companies that just take new hires to lunch on their first day and then expect them to dive in, we make new hires *slow down* and really get to know the business first.

Patient-experience advocate trainees spend two weeks in the classroom before advancing to a three-week on-the-job training session on the call center floor. During this second "transitional" phase, they acquire hands-on skills with the help of training support professionals who guide them through calls, minimize stress, answer questions, and help with escalations. The five weeks of new-hire training is generous by industry standards and costs the company roughly $7,000 per advocate. Once the new hires graduate, they are involved in regular recurrent training sessions for the rest of their careers. Our commitment to developing our employees doesn't stop there!

A Fun, Interactive Classroom

Our goal is to prepare employees for the job they have to do without boring them to death in the process. Games help make learning enjoyable, and they also introduce an element of healthy competition to the classroom. Even without prizes, games like Jeopardy, Pop-Up, Bang, and Bingo provide additional motivation and review opportunities. We have a lot of valuable fun playing Zip, Zap, Zop—a game based on sending cues across a circle of players using words and movement. There is always an element of mystery at first as to why we're playing the game and how it applies to the immediate lesson and the overall job. But the fit is perfect. The game requires you to think fast on your feet, listen actively, avoid unnecessary distractions, concentrate on what you are doing, follow guidelines, anticipate the communicator's need, use precise words, enunciate clearly, and above all, have fun! We want every call our patient-experience advocates take to be a Zip, Zap, Zop kind of call.

I always explain the rules in four to five steps, increasing the difficulty each time. When I add a new element, I ask the class to think about how this game applies to learning and how it applies to what they will soon be doing on the call center floor. In the beginning, they're a bit confused and they try to concentrate on learning the rules, but as we get going they start to see how the game requires them to execute several tasks that they'll be performing on the job. They also realize that the next two weeks will go by quickly and that they'll need to apply themselves 110 percent in order to get all they can out of the experience. A few months after each training session, I always have advocates come up to me in the hallway and tell me they're having a Zip, Zap, Zop kind of day. That alone gets me excited for the next class!

—*Jennifer*

Adults Don't Learn Like Children

While at times our classroom may look more like a preschool than a serious training environment, be assured that all our learning events are developed using the principles of adult learning theory.

Adults naturally like to have control over their learning environment, so we let new hires be active and creative to make sure that they learn better and faster. If there's a piece of lecture in the classroom curriculum that can possibly be turned into an activity, we do that to make the material more experiential. For example, a lesson about insurance including different types of insurance plans could be a two-hour lecture. Instead, we break students up into groups of four and give each group a book, a flip chart, and markers. Then we tell them, "You're about to leave this room and get creative. We want to see lots of color and pictures. Don't just copy the book on the page."

They go out and design posters, come back, put the posters up around the room, and teach one another. Without a single lecture, the trainees have become totally engaged. Since they create the lesson, they become fully invested in their own—and their coworkers'—knowledge of the subject.

It's also important to recognize that each person learns differently. In order to address the many different learning styles represented in each class, we employ a wide variety of learning methodologies. In a single class we might use videos, handouts, flip charts, lectures, discussion, hands-on exercises, notes, and illustrations to connect with the students and meet their learning needs.

The constant opportunity to be creative and to apply new skills and information to what we're doing is what makes it fun and exciting for our trainers. You may have delivered the same class ten times, but at the end of every session you realize there's a little something you can tweak. After a while, the tweaks accumulate and a once-established curriculum has effectively been revised—in real time. This constant freshening makes a huge difference to employee performance, and it's great to be able to come in every day and feel like we're serving our coworkers.

—Bob

Use Assessments

Don't be afraid to have high standards for all employees. People rise to your level of expectation. Properly designed assessments help you determine your employees' readiness to do their jobs. We set the expectations during the interview process, and each new hire understands that employment won't continue without making the grade. Is this harsh? Sure, but if we keep people who can't pass assessments, we're doing them—and us—a disservice. They would never be successful in our fast-paced environment.

We have five critical assessments during the new patient-experience advocate training process, and only two would be considered traditional formats. At the end of weeks one and two, trainees take tests that include multiple-choice, true–false, and fill-in-the-blank questions, along with completing real-life scenarios in our applications. During the third week, we assess their basic skill set. At this point, we expect them to have mastered our foundational skills—managing call flow and quality customer service. In weeks four and five, we expect them to show ongoing improvement in meeting set quality standards. If they don't pass all five assessments, they can't transition to their teams.

Never be afraid to say, "We were wrong." When you constantly assess trainees for skills, sometimes you'll realize that a person may not be as good a fit as they first seemed. We simply let trainees go if they can't get up to speed quickly enough or can't meet our stringent attendance standards. Again, it's better for both parties to identify any insurmountable shortcomings as quickly as possible.

Work Hard, Play Hard

New hires work hard, but we give them a lot of support and they're never isolated. We liven up classroom time with culture and educational visits from senior leaders, HR, and the employee culture committee, which assigns pairs in the Beryl Buddies program. Not all of our new hires have worked in call centers before, so it's gratifying when someone who has that experience will just "get it" one day and say, "You mean it's really OK for us to be *nice* to callers?" It's also interesting to observe the different reactions and responses to our culture. Each class has its own personality, but strong bonds and friendships always develop.

Call center training environments can be stressful. You've got one person at the front of the room going through the system in front of the class, ordinarily an intimidating way to learn. So we use scenarios and role-playing to solidify the material for the trainees and to help everyone get engaged. Trainers have developed a roster of memorable names and characters for different types of callers. When one pretends to be "Fran Tick" and acts extremely anxious as she's trying to find a doctor, it helps the classmates understand—very quickly—that a key part of their responsibility will be connecting frantic callers to proper care providers. Using creativity and nonthreatening humor, we're basically putting them on notice: "Hey, you're going to be taking some intense calls pretty soon, so get your heads in the game *right now*."

With so much information to digest, new hires find the humorous characters portrayed by trainers to be great memory aids. Trainees must also be prepared to take calls to hospitals from people who want a doctor for reasons that could be embarrassing to discuss with a stranger—everything from erectile dysfunction to transgender reassignment. They have to be ready to take those calls with maturity and sensitivity, so we have to desensitize them first by letting them laugh at the trainer. Once all the giggles are out, trainees know what they'll be up against on the phones and they're ready to handle difficult calls like pros. This light approach beats a stern lecture, hands down!

During the second week of training, each student gets up in front of the class to show their stuff. We call this drill "Head of the Class," and the students are both excited and nervous because they now become the advocate and must take a call from one of the many mystery personalities I portray. They may have to handle a proper southern belle, a "fast-talker," an elderly gentleman who is hard of hearing, an excited new mom, or a stereotypical "ditzy blond" who's not sure what kind of doctor she needs. As silly as it sounds, this kind of role-playing helps trainees think outside the box and spurs several new questions they haven't thought about until now.

One "Head of the Class" character was a French woman new to the States and looking for a doctor. The class thought my French accent was amusing, but they never thought they'd get a call like that. Two weeks later, several class members said, "You will not believe this, but I just got a call from a French lady who recently moved to America. She needed a doctor and I was able to help her!" You never know what kind of caller you're going to get or what they're going to need, so be prepared for anything. "Anything" happens every day!

—Jennifer

41

Earning Their Wings

By the time trainees get to on-the-job training (OJT)—the three-week transition phase—they've already developed great relationships and a solid team dynamic. Since our culture prizes relationship building, it's no surprise that we help trainees form strong bonds. To make sure they get to know everybody in their class, they are assigned a different seat every day.

On the first morning of OJT we set up a nice breakfast; trainees have their juice and their bagel and they're ready to go. They've absorbed a lot of information in the classroom, but some things won't start to "click" until they answer real calls. That's what they do for the next three weeks. We don't make them drink from the fire hose on the first day; they start out taking a subset of calls. As their comfort level rises, we gradually increase the number of clients they take calls for, and they're operating in the full queue at the end of week three. During the entire period, we've been taking them off the floor each day for an extra classroom hour of deeper dives into critical skills. This allows us to introduce client-specific information in a way they can retain and put into practice quickly. It's also an opportunity to address any negative trends we've noticed when they're taking live calls. We may also arrange to have a person sit with an outstanding advocate and listen in.

> *Our goal is to make every patient-experience advocate ready for work in five weeks. So the classroom and transition phase are like a flight simulator. They have five weeks to learn how to fly the plane well, and our operations managers and team leads tell us new hires are generally prepared quite well in those five weeks. Some are getting perfect scores on graded calls in their first week out on the floor!*
>
> *—Bob*

Continuous Support

To help provide development and support throughout the transition phase, we created our unique "LSP/TSP" program. The LSP—learning support professional—serves as a classroom assistant and subject matter expert during the two classroom weeks. This is always a "cream of the crop" advocate—someone with excellent attendance and quality scores, who is a true champion of the Beryl values. TSPs—training support professionals—serve as coaches, mentors, and help desk staff during the transition phase. These carefully selected, high-performing patient-experience advocates go through specialized training that prepares them for this new critical role—an excellent way to advance a career.

The LSP moves with the trainees from the classroom to the transition phase, where the TSPs join in. Throughout the transition phase, new coworkers are regularly taken off the phones by these professionals, who review scores and clarify our quality assessment criteria. If needed, they then coach the trainee in areas like diction, enunciation, and empathy—being able to convey a caring feeling over the phone with just voice tone or rate of speech. This process drives home performance expectations before trainees transition to their teams; they love the feedback and opportunity to ask questions.

Every business must train employees in industry-specific skill sets, and any time and ingenuity your training team can devote to these tricks of the trade is a great investment in your company's future. Multitasking—the ability to type and talk and search at the same time—is an essential skill for our advocates. If they can't do that, they lapse into silence on the phone, and coaches can help the advocate come up with personalized approaches that conform to our quality guidelines. We also make the coaching resource available to teams and individuals who have completed training.

How good are your coaches at passing on the craft wisdom of your business? Are they able to adjust these critical messages effectively for different members of your workforce?

Coaching is kind of like editing. A great editor can improve someone else's writing without distorting the author's voice. Our coaches let the advocate be himself or herself on a call, but what works for one advocate doesn't always work for another. The coach gives them the skills they need to manage a call without destroying the honest, personal touch and feel that is our company's trademark.

—Bob

Celebrate Success

At the end of the transition phase we encourage trainees to have a potluck before they graduate. The camaraderie is overwhelming and wonderful to see. We then have a graduation ceremony, which is much nicer and more elaborate than is common in our industry. We bring in food and an impressive throng of coworkers show up to applaud the graduates.

We introduce each patient-experience advocate individually and showcase special talents and accomplishments—a compliment from a customer or a perfect test score. Some will tell a story about their trainers or give them a gift. There's a lot of "warm and fuzzy" to it and it's a great way to send people off into their careers. The graduates get a nice graduation certificate, and their team lead is there to welcome them to their team.

We try to jazz up each ceremony with a few fun surprises so they won't become tedious over time. One class had a high concentration of style-conscious young ladies, many of whom dressed up in cocktail attire and feather boas for their graduation. Another class wore camouflage and played the theme song from *M*A*S*H*. However, other classes have preferred a traditional graduation ceremony with cake and punch. The important thing is to match the celebration to the personality of the class.

When asked about their classroom experience following their graduation, coworkers always talk about how much fun they had in the classroom and how much they learned in such a short period of time. They appreciate the activities we develop to make the learning process as painless as possible.

From day one, we welcome the trainees into our classrooms with music and pom-poms and cheers from people throughout the building. All the trainers introduce themselves and share a little bit of personal information. The bonding continues for five weeks until we celebrate their graduation to their teams. It's an exciting, atypical approach that makes the graduates feel important and valued.

—Bob

Be Flexible

All our team members in the Center for Learning and Growth are well-rounded and are as comfortable developing curriculum as they are delivering it. In a fast-paced environment, we frequently have to develop a course and then turn right around and teach it. Flexibility is every bit as important as creativity, and immediate needs take priority.

For new accounts with unusual service requirements, we'll develop specialized training and bring the designated advocate team into the classroom so they can learn these unique twists, practice on them, ask questions, and give us more feedback. One unusually complex account has a dedicated instructional designer who plans and delivers all training for the client. Finally, new product launches and the concurrent client input can also necessitate new training.

Quality training materials take time to develop. For each hour of classroom training, the industry standard is between thirty and forty hours of development effort. We're close to that average on some projects, but when deadlines are pressing we can design a solid hour of classroom instruction in anywhere from eight to twenty hours. Each project has its own requirements, and clients sign off on development estimates before we start.

Perpetual Education

After graduation, our quality assurance team will grade patient-experience advocate calls each month, and we'll deliver recurrent training where we see opportunities for improvement. The goal is always to provide advocates with the immediate tools they need, and a lot of science goes into choosing the topics.

A member of the operations team does trend analysis and identifies where call advocates may be struggling. When this occurs, we work to identify whether the issue is skills or behavior. If it's a skills gap, we have to develop and deliver training to address the need quickly. If we have a ton of information that people need to get up to speed with right away, this kind of recurrent training session may end up being a straightforward lecture.

Account managers are also quick to let us know if clients are voicing concerns, and our operations VP meets frequently with large sample groups of advocates to get feedback. These sessions often result in additional training or support materials being developed for advocates. We may be scheduled to do a "positive customer communication" unit for every advocate on the floor, but if we detect a trend in one group that needs a quick fix, they'll get the urgent specialized training instead.

To be a premium service provider, you have to commit to the concept of perpetual learning. Training is ultimately what turns culture into performance. Without it, a culture program can end up being nothing but parties and talk. Our recurrent training program can mean twenty-four three-hour classes in a month for a single trainer. That's 24 times she has to make sure she has a room, 24 times she has to prep all the materials, and 24 times she has to consult with workforce management to make sure everybody who needs the class is scheduled. It's very unusual for trainers to deliver that kind of customer service.

Don't Forget Your Support Staff

Most companies do a fair job of developing employees who handle their core business, but when was the last time you offered a class that could benefit your finance and IT departments? We think every person in the organization deserves an opportunity to stretch and grow their skills, but this doesn't mean that trainers have to become experts in cost accounting and Microsoft product installations. When we learn of the need for classes like that, we happily recommend training vendors that focus on those specialized areas. While their jobs are vastly different, both a cost accountant and an IT professional can benefit from learning how to interpret someone's behavioral style or to refine their presentation skills.

By identifying core competencies that apply throughout the organization, we've created a suite of courses that are applicable no matter what role you play on our support staff. While most of these courses are developed in-house, we do occasionally purchase curricula from industry-leading providers. Center staffers always deliver the courses, creating a winning mix of nationally recognized expertise and Beryl experience.

During a recent time management class, a participant came up to me and expressed his frustrations about not being organized. He felt more reactive than proactive, and most nights he was having to stay late. He said he was really looking forward to getting some "time management relief." When the class concluded, he was genuinely excited about putting the techniques to work.

Three weeks later, he approached me with tears in his eyes. He could hardly express his gratitude for the results he saw in his personal life. Not only did he feel more organized and proactive at work, but his five-year-old daughter had told him the night before that it was good to have her daddy home again to tuck her into bed. I realized that what we teach at work impacts home lives as well.

—Bob

Career Development

Every employee understands that he or she can grow in a career here. Patient-experience advocates know they can apply to be cross-trained and hired onto more demanding, better-paying accounts, and we prominently publicize the series of job bands and promotional opportunities. Several patient-experience advocates have moved into important positions in our support staff, and we applaud any ambitious employee who raises her hand and says, "I'm willing to learn! What do you want me to do?"

We strongly encourage participation in the weekend classes we offer on a variety of topics. Come in on your day off and invest in yourself! A regularly offered and always popular class is "Interviewing Skills and Résumé Writing"—how to dress, how to speak in an interview, and all the due-diligence tasks that tend to impress a hiring manager. We've had as many as sixty people attend one of these sessions on their own time. Some organizations would be afraid to offer this class for fear of teaching employees how to leave the company. We feel obligated in order to help coworkers advance internally.

Our commitment to career development throughout the company is also reflected in the creation of a career development task force. The group focuses on all roles, helping to further refine career paths and making recommendations to senior leadership. Even outside the official training arena, our culture provides employees with opportunities to show the organization what they can do. When our "green team" rolled out the Beryl Earth Initiative, one patient-experience advocate gave an amazingly polished PowerPoint presentation to a group of senior leaders who took note of that individual's potential.

Every month, the training department sends out tips to the support staff and advocates. The tips can cover everything from time management, social styles, and presentation skills to active listening, questioning techniques, and proactive customer service. We usually get all kinds of responses. Many of the staff e-mail back to say how they "need to pay more attention in certain areas of their daily workday," or that they "hadn't thought of that as a resource," or that they "will start applying the advice right away."

Recently, we realized that people are applying the monthly tips at home as well as at work. I've had several people say things like, "Hey, I used your listening tip this weekend with my boys and it worked! I really heard what they were trying to say and we ended up resolving an issue that would have usually turned into an argument." Or, "The advice you gave on questioning techniques really helped me with my wife. I was able to figure out what she really wanted and needed. Thank you!" It's funny how often what we learn at work benefits us in our personal lives. When we hear these stories we know we have succeeded in improving the lives of our coworkers, both personally and professionally.

—Jhan

Make It Count

It's easy to fall in the trap of just counting the number of people you train each year and calling a big number a success. While that may be a just measure of how efficient your training department is, does it measure the effectiveness of the training itself? Start small by asking for feedback from your trainees to find out what they liked and didn't like in the course. This information will allow you to constantly refine and revise your training. As you become more comfortable, start measuring how your training is positively impacting the organization. Publicize this information on a regular basis to reinforce the message that your company is a learning organization.

Shout it from the rooftops!

Tips and Tools

1. ## Make a system-wide commitment to learning and growth.
   - Integrate immediate training needs into a broader culture of lifelong learning and personal improvement.
   - Balance new information against preserving traditional values.
   - Constantly assess and refresh all curricula.
   - Make the financial investment to provide full-spectrum training—from new hires' to executives' development.
   - Dedicate an entire day of new-hire training to your culture and values.
   - Invest in design; quality training materials take time to develop.

2. ## Experiment with classroom techniques.
   - Add guest presenters from senior leadership and your culture committee to keep students from feeling isolated.
   - Change seating daily to encourage bonding.
   - Let trainers personalize their curricula and presentations.
   - Make sure to incorporate fun, self-learning, and relationship building into training.
   - Use memorable materials and experiential techniques, such as:
     a. Scenarios
     b. Role-playing
     c. Humor
     d. Games
     e. Stories
     f. Self-learning activities
   - Employ pass–fail assessments and a stringent attendance policy.

- Celebrate trainee graduations with personalized ceremonies. Send them off with a bang!

3. **Don't neglect on-the-job training.**
   - Make constant skill–fit assessments through regular quality and performance measurements.
   - Offer remedial coaching as needed in essential skill sets—hard and soft.
   - Coaching is nurture—not discipline.
   - Only the most accomplished employees should be given the honor of coaching.

4. **Recurrent training is critically important.**
   - Retouch employees as frequently as needed.
   - Coordinate closely with operations and account services.
   - Poll employees in focus groups on their perceived needs.
   - Be flexible—agility is key in addressing changing organizational needs.

5. **Don't forget your support staff.**
   - Offer development courses in key organizational competencies.
   - Partner with nationally recognized leaders in subjects where you don't have in-house expertise.

6. **Provide career path options and promote career development.**
   - Publicize job bands and promotional opportunities.
   - Offer weekend classes to encourage employees to invest in their own development.
   - Make opportunities available internally for the honing of executive skills.

7. **Make it count.**
   - Use surveys to solicit feedback after courses are taught.
   - Measure the *impact* training has on your organization, not the number of "butts in seats."

4

Communication

By Jennifer Mills, Lara Morrow, and Lance Shipp

You've probably read many chapters of many books with this title. But this one is written by some great communicators at Beryl. Lance is our chief operating officer, and he is always committed to making sure our employees know why they're doing what they do, how it connects to the vision, and what's in it for them if they help us get there. Jennifer heads the communications task force of the Better Beryl Bureau. Lara ties it all together to make sure that our messages are getting to all levels of the organization. You'll learn in this chapter that communication must be done in multiple mediums and with great repetition. This isn't about announcements . . . it is about consistent two-way dialogue.

—Paul

In business and relationships alike, poor communication is the root of much frustration and many regrets. Most honest managers will admit that their organizations could do a better job with internal communication. A discipline you always have to work at and seldom perfect, internal communication is worth every ounce of effort you can spare.

Transparency has been the foundational principle of our program from the start. When your business environment is transparent, employees can see any difference between what you're saying and what you're doing. That's a good thing! The minute people suspect that management is withholding information or not being totally honest with them, loyalty, productivity, and customer service start to slide. Quicker than you might expect, these slides will affect your profits. By consistently honoring the transparency principle, you'll overcome the "show me" sensibility that tends to prevail in a workforce and reap real benefits as a result.

Transparency keeps people honest by making it almost impossible for them to engage in improprieties or propagate rumors. In a relatively small, intensely interactive company, it also reinforces approachability and the open-door policy. These three tactics all end up working together as truth mechanisms and make it easy for people at different levels of the organization to know what's going on and to find out almost instantaneously if anything is out of whack.

Basic open-book management techniques are a great place to start. We have been posting our financials on our intranet for years. We don't include line-item budget details, but it's a clear profit–loss statement with a summary of how we're doing against budget and how the current year is shaping up in comparison to the previous year. This financial snapshot is also a standard slide in quarterly town hall meetings attended by every employee. Our bonus programs are in large part based on financial performance, so there's a significant motivational effect to making sure everyone knows exactly where the company stands.

When you support an open-book approach with a coordinated set of internal communication tools and programs, transparency begins to become a reality. Our list of tools includes different kinds of communication: input, output, one-way, two-way, formal, and informal. Be creative and persistent, and make sure your tools are all relevant. A good communication program is always evolving.

The key to our program is making sure it's having an effect and, if it's not, figuring out what we can do to communicate better. Since coworkers know we're always refreshing our communication channels, they're quick to suggest new ideas.

—Lance

Print Is Not Dead

It's easy in the age of Twitter to overlook old-school communication tools, but still *way* too early to equate employee magazines with cuneiform tablets. When internal print pieces suck—as they frequently do—the blame lies with inept messengers, not the time-honored medium. For cost-efficient morale enhancement, it's hard to beat a cleverly designed internal print piece that directly—and cleverly—supports who you are and what your company is about.

It took us years to fine-tune *Beryl Life*, the twelve- to fifteen-page full-color magazine published bimonthly by our marketing department. The cover logo pays tribute to the classic *Life* magazine, whose original statement of purpose we admire: "We wish to have some fun . . ." A typical issue of *Beryl Life* does include a dose of timely industry and marketplace information, but the focus is overwhelmingly on the human face of our business—informative, photo-rich articles by Beryl people about Beryl people.

A running storyline lately involves the "Beryl bears" we hand out as promotional knickknacks. Employees take these stuffed animals on their vacations, and the magazine is constantly running pictures of our little toy mascot on the Eiffel Tower, the Great Wall of China, the Empire State Building, and in more exotic locales. This feature is so popular that some employees are probably planning their next vacation trips around teddy bear photo shoots.

In the magazine's "Beryl Cares" section, we post celebratory announcements for employees about any positive things going on in their lives. Just a photo and brief explanation of each happy event—new home, new baby, son gets married, daughter wins a choir award. Other popular sections cover our community outreach programs and updates on what's coming up in the culture world.

Beryl Life is a time-consuming project. The minute one issue goes out the team starts working on the next one. The magazine resided in HR before, and has been divvied up in the past via committee to give different contributors responsibility for different sections. Ultimately, we found that it made better sense to have one person planning and organizing the contributors. We print 500 copies of each issue and mail 350 copies directly to the homes of employees. The rest are distributed to select customers or set out in the lobby and other areas for people visiting the facility.

We want family members to see and read about what's going on here. The magazine serves as an extension of the Beryl family into these households, and coworkers tell us their spouses and kids look forward to every issue. Human beings simply thrive on positive, personal exposure and recognition. They love looking at pictures of themselves and their friends and keeping up with good things happening in their immediate world. This print piece reinforces everything we're doing and presents everything management has been talking about in an attractive, friendly format.

Companies that don't think twice about spending serious money on brochures would not match our investment in *Beryl Life*. But year after year—for a measly 1 percent response rate—they print and mail out expensive marketing materials, then hand their employees a cheap newsletter that promptly ends up in the trash, unread. Our Circle of Growth philosophy considers it foolish to scrimp like this on internal communication. We want to make sure we're constantly building up employee loyalty, and we know smart print efforts work well. At one point we tried to convert this publication to online-only but were overwhelmed by requests to "bring it back to print."

Beryl TV

We have flat-screen TVs throughout the facility in high-traffic areas like the employee break room, main hallway, and lobby. What we have come to call "Beryl TV" is not a TV channel per se, but a series of eye-catching, high-tech messages programmed with graphics that enables us to communicate whatever we want.

When clients are sitting in the lobby they can watch a screen scrolling employee birthdays, client anniversaries, and a list of cities around the country from which live calls are originating. We promote community outreach events the company is supporting and display our core values and the names of recognition award winners. The feed gets updated every week and different TVs can display different things.

Beryl TV is another way to make sure people know what's going on, and it can also be a good morale booster. When two employees were horsing around before a recent holiday party, our creative director captured their little song-and-dance routine on video. Five minutes later, people were watching it on Beryl TV. For the next few days, this comical little clip added a lot to the festive mood in the office.

The Whole World in Their Hands

We couldn't have the culture we do without our intranet, which connects the entire organization to a variety of communication tools. Everything people want to be informed about lives on the Gemstar home page: employee birthdays and anniversaries, client anniversaries, department updates, and links to commonly used forms. A different employee picture comes up every time you click on the home page; a different brand story and recognition program nomination pops up every time you log in. You can click on logos arrayed across the top of the screen to find out what's happening with the employee culture committee, wellness and environmental programs, and seven other areas of interest. We put it all at their fingertips and make it super easy to search and use.

There are three popular "reactive" communication forums on the home page that let coworkers initiate dialogues with management. "Ask Paul" gives employees a chance to direct questions to the CEO. A recent example: "Hi Paul! I know that Beryl is really into giving back to the community. I realize that there is a homeless gentleman that lives in his car near Taco Bell. Can we do anything to help his situation?" An "Ask Lindy" forum lets employees air out concerns with the operations vice president, and the "Suggestion Box" is monitored by the culture director. Suggestions can be random, but they allow everyone the opportunity to express their personal interests, whatever these might be: "Ever thought about changing the colors in the call center to bright yellow and dark green or some other colors?" All of the questions and answers within these venues of back-and-forth communication are immediately posted to the intranet for everyone to see. All three forums provide management with steady, valuable input and help us gauge morale.

> *One of our admin people reads Ask Paul, Ask Lindy, and Suggestion Box every morning. She says it's how she stays plugged in with what's going on.*
>
> *—Lara*

Anybody who knows how to build a webpage can mimic Gemstar with a simple program like FrontPage. It helps to have someone like our creative director in the background to assist tech-challenged execs with posting information. We deputized half a dozen additional employees to update information for their own departments—birthdays, new policies, performance incentives, etc. Spreading out the responsibility this way is a big plus.

Centralized Communication

When an organization has so much going on it can often seem like communication overload. We started to hear that there were so many e-mails that it was hard to keep up. The BBB Communications Subcommittee leader started a weekly e-mail to staff called "What's Going On." She collects important information from all managers, including important events, contests, meetings, and projects. She summarizes all the information in one formal e-mail and sends it to staff.

It became obvious that we had a need for a better, more consistent way to communicate with our staff. They were becoming overwhelmed by the multiple e-mails promoting events, deadlines, or opportunities. We really had no way of keeping track of the different events. I started by taking the multiple e-mails that were sent out during a week and condensing them into one comprehensive e-mail. As soon as I sent that first "What's Going On" e-mail, I was overwhelmed with the amount of positive feedback I received. Patient-experience advocates really appreciated the new streamlined communication and thanked me for making their e-mails more manageable within the time constraints of their position. Now, instead of multiple e-mails throughout the week, they get to look forward to one e-mail every Friday!
—Jennifer

The Personal Touch

We've also had success with proactive communication tools we send out to employees in e-mail format. In his monthly CEO letter, Paul usually shares some personal information and a customer service touch point, then addresses anything going on in the company that he feels is noteworthy. The letters are short and sweet and always include a recent photo of his kids, which goes a long way to reinforce the personal connection.

"Did Ya Know" e-mails from our chief operating officer address important topics but often use lighthearted trivia to tie in a message and make it memorable. Buried in these unscheduled, impromptu texts, it's not unusual to find messages like: "The first five people to e-mail me back get Starbucks gift cards." The e-mails are easy to read, not overly long, and include some kind of pasted-in photo or graphic to break up the text and add visual appeal. While more formal corporate communication tends to flow in one eye and out the other, a good "Did Ya Know" will have a certain dorky charm that makes it more like a note from a personal friend. Here's a sample "Did Ya Know" that really showcases how important industry information can be streamlined to be better and more easily absorbed:

Did Ya Know: We're going to Oz!

What is "The Oz Principle" training all about? A year ago, Beryl agreed to add a fifth core value—Commitment to Accountability. Now, core values aren't something that can be mandated. They need to reflect those things that we as an organization agree upon and believe are important. Core values influence almost every aspect of our lives: our choices, our responses to others, our aesthetic preferences, our objectives, and our sense of ethics and morality. They motivate us before we achieve a goal and determine how satisfied we will feel once we attain that goal. Simply put, goals are what we want; values are what we think are important. Beryl has been recognized as an award-winning great place to work for a long time. That only defines part of who we are and what we think is important. Sometimes the negative effect of being a great place to work is that some people get a sense of entitlement or place "fun" over performance. How many excuses have you personally heard about why things didn't get done or why they went wrong? We want a culture that focuses on the solutions—not the excuses.

Did ya know these are real accident reports (excuses) filed with insurance companies:

- Coming home, I drove into the wrong house and collided with a tree I don't have.
- The guy was all over the road. I had to swerve a number of times before I hit him.
- My car was legally parked as it backed into the other vehicle.
- A pedestrian hit me and went under my car.
- I had been shopping for plants all day and was on my way home. As I reached an intersection a hedge sprang up, obscuring my vision, and I did not see the other car!

These are fun to read but they all reflect a common theme: a lack of accountability. The Oz Principle training will provide us with a common outlook and language with which to discuss accountability. You will learn phrases like "below the line" thinking related to whining and excuse making and "above the line" thinking focused on solutions. You will be given tips and tools to make this an everyday part of your thinking and conversation. The core value of Commitment to Accountability is something we need to live every day and take a sense of pride in knowing that we are walking the talk on a daily basis. It doesn't happen overnight. I believe we will all benefit from and enjoy this training as we learn to "See It. Own It. Solve It. Do It."

While people are looking for the fun stuff, they're also reading everything you wanted them to read. And I can't send one out without getting up to ten comments back. Planning and execution is not a burden; you can do two in one week and then not do one for a month and a half.

—*Lance*

Lay It on Us

The third proactive e-mail campaign is the company's employee opinion survey, distributed every November by a web survey generator. The survey is comprehensive and incorporates relevant areas of interest we've borrowed over the years from applications for different Best Places to Work competitions. While many questions are phrased in a "rate from one to five" format, we deliberately ask a lot of open-ended questions and welcome detailed written responses.

The senior leadership team reviews all feedback, looking for trends we need to keep an eye on in the year ahead. The culture director will then coordinate focus groups to address anything else requiring scrutiny or improvement. People from all over the organization make recommendations and a task force determines solutions. Every employee is sent an invitation to apply for the task force, which meets monthly to discuss the top five concerns of the focus groups. These can be minor things, like adding spell-check to an application, or more serious requests for policy changes.

Some companies utilize surveys but never talk about the results or any intended response. We constantly communicate what we're doing, what we've done, and the resultant improvements. Knowing that their input will be read and addressed, people are more honest. And there's deliberate precommunication to make sure they feel safe laying their true feelings on the line. The culture director hammers home the confidential nature of the poll: "Here's how a web survey generator works. Here are the screens we get to see, and here's the technical reason why we can't trace your answers back to you and chop your head off if you raise hell about something." It's an effective demonstration of our commitment to transparency, and it gives employees an abiding sense of security.

The opinion survey is our second-best morale measurement after turnover. Performance evaluations for senior leadership team members take employee satisfaction into account, and compensation and bonus plans are directly affected by the results of this ongoing litmus test.

Town Halls

Employees appreciate regular opportunities to hear what's going on in the company straight from the mouth of management, up close and personal. We take the time to stage quarterly, hour-long town hall meetings because we want to make sure everybody has a clear picture of what's happening internally and externally. We set an upbeat mood by playing music as people enter and leave, and AV support is frequently humorous. We also have a popular drawing where we give away nice prizes for our recognition program.

Sessions start with a standard twenty-minute update on customers, strategies, events, and other topical concerns. Once we've told the group what we think is important for them to know, we encourage them to ask us whatever they want to know. No matter how fascinating your company's market position may be, most employees naturally want to know how developments will affect them personally.

Live two-way communication exposes management to tough questions. You never really know what people will ask when they raise their hands, a fact that has made for some interesting sessions. To anticipate concerns, we pay close attention to feedback we've been getting on the intranet forums, and the culture director does a quick poll of senior managers right before each town hall: "What are the hot topics right now? What are you hearing?" So we can often preemptively address a few beefs head-on with our presentation. Operational and HR issues come up frequently, so we always have reps from those departments on hand to provide details.

In a good session, people feel comfortable enough to ask questions so you can get a transparent dialogue going with honest answers. Sometimes the answer is yes, sometimes the answer is no. A lot of times the answer is: "You know, that's a good idea. I'm not sure what we can do about it, but we'll find out and get back to you." We write down every question and post them all on the intranet for people who missed the session. And if you make any promises, you have to notify the responsible manager and set things in motion to make sure you have satisfactory follow-up at the next town hall.

> *When we do our first town hall at the beginning of the year, we always say: "These were the issues you told us we needed to look at in the last employee opinion survey, and here's what we've done. These were your top comments, and these were your remarks on things we need to work on. You wanted spell-check in the call-handling application; we gave it to you.*

You wanted Dr Pepper in the break room; we gave it to you.
You wanted us to review the attendance policy, and we did."

—*Lara*

Scheduling quarterly sessions can be tough if, like us, you run multiple shifts or cannot pull everyone away from their duties simultaneously. To cover everyone, we may have two or three sessions in the morning one day, then two sessions the next afternoon. Pulling people off the phones means lost revenue, but enhanced communication is definitely the best thing for the company long-term.

Group Meetings

Strategy and operational meetings, department and team meetings, scheduled meetings and meetings on the fly—what organization doesn't struggle with these demands? In spite of an understood policy—"Let's not meet to meet again"—our managers still spend much of the day sitting, listening, and working their way through agendas. To make sure inevitable meetings don't eat up the clock, we rely on brutal-facts-only communication. This aggressive form of transparency takes some getting used to, but it does help things get done.

Every meeting participant is there to address issues as they exist. If you can't do that, you're wasting everyone's time and keeping problems from getting solved. Participants are expected to talk to one another in a way that breaks down silos, and we don't leave the room until things are completely hashed out, even when discussions start to get tense. An honest quarrel in front of your peers is infinitely preferable to politics and backstabbing behind closed doors.

Brutal-facts-only communication has livened up—and salvaged—some of our usually deadly dull operational meetings.

For example, the operational committee deals with the logistical nuts and bolts of the business—project reviews, software upgrades, updates on new customers coming onboard—but we also vet new business opportunities. In one instance, sales team reps had developed a bad habit of presenting any lead they could find. After a series of meetings in which brutally factual inquiries shredded every bogus prospect, the reps are now much more disciplined about the opportunities they submit and much less precious time is wasted.

Be honest about the meeting itself. We try to end each meeting with a plus–minus takedown. What was good about it, and what was bad? Did we have the right folks in the room (i.e., only the people required to make the decision, without excluding anyone with critical information)? Could the meeting have been combined with another scheduled meeting? You can't do this analysis every time, but you should be asking questions like this frequently and either abolishing meetings or modifying formats as a result. Everybody should be educated about meeting optimization and should strive to achieve it.

Finally, in any group, camaraderie and respect are the keys to effective communication. In our senior leadership meetings, it's not seen as a sign of weakness to ask for help on a challenging project. Junior managers are routinely included in strategy meetings so they can better explain the company's goals to their teams. And even in a ten-minute stand-up meeting, team leaders make it a point to recognize personal efforts and jobs well done.

One-to-Ones

The number one reason people leave a company is a poor relationship with their manager, with poor communication a common factor in the equation. Our managers are required to meet one-to-one with every team member at least bimonthly.

Most have the individual meetings one week and a group meeting the next. One-to-ones are vitally important to ensuring regular conversations, building up relationships, and keeping people on track with their priorities. The ultimate goal: no surprises by the time you get to your midyear or quarterly reviews. You should be addressing any and all issues along the way.

We keep the meeting format simple. It's basically: "Let's sit down and talk about what's going on. Here's what our group is doing this week and how we're supporting that. What are your priorities? Is there anything I need to know about?" To keep the coworker up to speed, the manager will often attach a list of the coworker's objectives at the bottom of the review form to keep these front and center. Conversely, the coworker is free to communicate with the manager: "Here's what's going on with me personally" or "I'm falling behind because another department isn't supporting us. Is there anything we can do about that?"

For the scheduling issues noted earlier, it is a headache for us to consistently implement one-to-ones with patient-experience advocates—our most vocal constituency. It's a struggle with traveling salespeople, too. But to the extent we fail to maintain this discipline, nagging miscommunication will invariably cause much bigger headaches down the road.

I have weekly one-to-ones with my direct reports simply because things are moving so fast. And I actually look forward to them. Everybody is so busy it can be hard to catch up if we don't set a time to sit down and talk. Do they happen every single week? No. Do they happen the majority of the time? Absolutely.

—Lance

Myth Busting

Listening is the heart of communication, and individual opinions matter tremendously. That's why we take the time for regular employee "Lunches with Lance and Lara" and the "Chat n' Chews" described in the chapter on leadership. In the general category of personal opinions, rumors deserve special attention. It is simply astonishing how far afield a single person's mouth and imagination can run, how quickly such misinformation can spread, and how easily it can end up distracting an entire workforce.

The good news: it doesn't take long to learn about rumors in a transparent organization. Members of our employee culture committee are a great resource, and queries to "Ask Paul" and "Ask Lindy" can be great clues. Thanks to the open-door policy, someone can simply end up sitting in your office, saying, "I just overheard the craziest conversation and thought you ought to know about it."

As information can flow in through different channels, we have multiple ways to address rumors and we try to be selective about the best venue. If we feel everyone on staff needs clarification, we may devote a slide in a town hall presentation or a "Did Ya Know" e-mail to a specific rumor. We're blunt in these "myth buster" updates: "Here's a couple hot rumors going around. Now, let's talk about fact versus fiction." We may bring it up as a discussion topic during a scheduled lunch with two or three people: "Hey, have you guys heard this? Let me tell you what's going on in this area." Or we'll hold a group meeting with team leaders and say, "This is the tall tale making the rounds; these are the facts you need to explain to your teams."

Disseminating relevant information and setting facts straight are unavoidable policing actions in a transparent organization. Put the truth out there calmly and with zero sense of indignation because there's usually an innocent explanation for rumors. And if the people starting the rumors didn't know all the pertinent facts—if they only had a piece of the story regarding an important matter—whose fault is that in a company that prides itself on stellar internal communications?

We don't see the communication tools we use as optional. We have so many cross-functional teams, and our pace of operations is so quick, that it's imperative for the left hand to always know what the right hand is doing. To make sure we all know what's going on, everybody needs to be comfortable talking to any other coworker. As the different communication building blocks support one another, over time you start to develop critical mass and the kind of genuine transparency that translates into a competitive edge.

Honestly, we probably wouldn't get a unanimous yes if we asked everybody in the company right now if there are no silos or communication barriers here. But everybody can see that efforts are being made to tear down the walls.

Tips and Tools

1. **Make transparency the foundation of your program.**
   - Set the tone by posting financials on the intranet.
   - Share financial information and strategic direction in quarterly meetings.
   - Support this outreach with a set of communication tools.
   - Address bad news head-on. (Good news is easy!)
   - Be honest.

2. **Invest in an employee magazine or newsletter.**
   - Make it high quality, informative, and people-focused.
   - Include lots of positive recognition and exposure.
   - Mail it to coworkers' homes.
   - Orient some articles to families.

3. **Start your own TV channel.**
   - Put flat-screen TVs in high-traffic areas.
   - Use programmed "crawl" text and graphics.
   - Try occasional fun videos.

4. **Leverage your intranet.**
   - A simple FrontPage site will do.
   - Array six or more communication tools on the home page:
     a. "Ask the CEO," "Ask the COO," etc.
     b. "Suggestion Box"
     c. Nominations for a recognition program
     d. Wellness and environmental programs
     e. Brand stories
   - Spread out update responsibilities among departments.

5. **Proactive e-mail campaigns can be friendly and fun.**
   - CEO letters provide an inclusionary atmosphere.
   - "Did Ya Know" from the COO can make relating information quick and engaging.

6. **Employee opinion surveys remove roadblocks in effective communication.**
   - An easy-to-use tool is an annual, comprehensive web questionnaire.
   - Focus groups review results and a task force determines solutions.
   - Keep everyone posted on progress and results.

7. **Town halls create company-wide transparency.**
   - Hold a quarterly open forum session: twenty minutes for briefing, forty minutes of Q&A.
   - Music and humorous AV support helps.
   - Have HR and operations personnel on deck for backup.
   - Post all Q&A topics online afterward.

8. **Group meetings need to speed up productivity, not slow it down.**
   - Brutal-facts-only communication saves time.
   - Educate everyone on meeting optimization.
   - Emphasize camaraderie.

9. **Use small "Chat n' Chew"-type lunch meetings as a preventative measure.**
   - Make them conversational (three or four people over food).
   - Ask your guests what's on their minds.
   - Use the occasion to disseminate information and set the record straight.

10. One-to-ones can keep individual performance levels high.
    - Set up bimonthly reviews with a simple, standardized format.
    - Be disciplined and adhere to a schedule.

11. "Myth busting" is a necessary action.
    - Monitor rumors carefully.
    - Choose the appropriate venue for a response.
    - Disseminate factual rebuttals in a good-natured way.

5

The Mechanics of Fun

By Melissa Barnes, Melissa Bloom, Lindy Butterfield, Greg Williams, Elaine McCullough, and Patrick Gonzales

How can fun be "mechanical"? Because it is a planned and executed part of our culture. In this chapter, you'll hear from the "Two Melissas," longtime leaders in our account management team and the first to plan a fun event or get their coworkers in the mood for a good parade around the call center floor. Greg is an operations manager who is not afraid to show his dance moves at our annual Gong Show. Lindy is our VP of operations, someone who is responsible for all of our day-to-day operations and metrics, but who also will be the first one cooking hot dogs outside and serving them to her team. You'll also hear from two front-line coworkers, Patrick and Elaine, whose personal stories you'll enjoy. In this chapter, you'll learn how a fun culture not only impacts employees but has a measured impact on our relationships with our customers.

—Paul

Considering the tooth-and-claw, dog-eat-dog reality of modern business competition, what manager in his or her right mind would waste a second of precious time considering "fun" as a strategic option? Pushed into a corner, most managers will admit that morale can dictate performance, but the general approach to enhancing productivity today is all numbers and no nonsense.

This is unfortunate, because Beryl has documented a direct connection between the "fun and events" component of our culture and our unique profitability—six times higher than the industry average. Fun helps drive our loyalty and dedication, promotes cross-functional team building, and significantly advances other operational objectives like low turnover and a 96 percent customer retention rate—so much so that we're comfortable in insisting that you'd be foolish not to at least experiment with injecting a little strategic lightheartedness into your own operation. When an employee has fun at work, they're much more likely to pass that positive energy to customers and clients.

Before we came to Beryl, all four of us had lengthy careers in operations in much more traditional corporate cultures: staffing agencies, healthcare operations, and the airline industry, to name a few. Each company had its own culture, and we're not here to proclaim them good or bad. In most corporate environments, culture is simply what's expected. Disney and McDonald's are both profitable companies, with their cultures worlds apart. Staunch, formal professionalism worked fairly well for our former employers, and the fun family formula works beautifully for us now. Since the occasional need for affection and relaxation is hardwired into human beings, it's a formula that works in most contexts.

The following points are the most exportable truths we've learned about the value of fun as we continue to fine-tune the formula. First, we take a look at applications of the concept in the operations department—the heart of Beryl. Then we see how fun is a critical component to how the account services department manages relationships, both internally among our employees and externally with our clients.

Fun and Operations

Operations is responsible for 240 people: patient-experience advocates, team leads, workforce management, and the quality assurance team. According to Beryl's Circle of Growth philosophy, the morale of this main body of troops—70 percent of all personnel—contributes mightily to the company's bottom line.

Like other managers in the company, we feel obliged to help the culture team motivate our people. We work hand in hand with the culture director to make sure she knows where we stand with our service metrics and how to determine optimal hours, days, weeks, and months for company-wide events. No event is worth doing if we can only let ten people participate—this can quickly become a demotivator—and some time slots just don't work for us. During those times, it's now clearly understood that operations literally cannot play. However, our forecasters enable us to optimize our available time to schedule and participate in cultural events, training, and other fun things.

In addition to company-wide programs like the Halloween carnival, branding initiatives, and community events, operations does its own monthly incentives and contests focused on performance stats, with the specific jobs of patient-experience advocates and team leads in mind. Careful temperature-taking is important. We get together regularly with the thirteen team leads to review scorecard data and identify immediate performance shortcomings that promptly become the focus of the contests.

Contest themes always match the incentive (e.g., winners of the March Madness tournament get to go to an NBA game). In the summer, we offer tickets to outdoor facilities like Six Flags and Hurricane Harbor, as well as "cool" indoor options like movie tickets. The incentives aren't just for recognition. They have to drive performance—and they don't have to be expensive to do that. Some rewards don't cost much at all, like having a team lead, ops manager, or even the ops VP take calls for an employee who wins extra break time or a lunch off campus.

While department-wide events predominate, as a bottom-up culture we give the team leads a lot of latitude to design their own events. About every three months, each team lead will focus their incentive—which we have to approve—on a specific metric that is challenging that team. If a team lead wants to do his or her own thing, we need to know by the fifteenth of the prior month.

> *Fun and excitement is contagious because everybody else hears us talking about the contest and they want to get involved, too.*
>
> —*Elaine*

Our last March Madness competition is a great example of how these competitions tie directly to metrics. March is always a crazily busy month for us in terms of call volume, and since we were somewhat short-staffed this year we knew that a motivational edge would be a big help. We communicated the theme and the target metrics to the team leads, and they disseminated the information to their patient-experience advocates. A competitive spirit took hold immediately, and the team leads kept advocates motivated by the challenge throughout the month.

Teams in the first bracket competed against one another on schedule adherence. The goal was 95 percent, and six teams managed 96 percent or better. The themes of the second and third bracket competitions were reducing unproductive time and maximizing attendance; quality was the focus of the Final Four. Thanks in no small part to the competition, we were able to increase productivity and make sure coworkers weren't taking unnecessary sick days. We handled the call volume perfectly and had a lot of fun in the process.

We compete against each other in events, and this rivalry creates strong camaraderie within the teams. We really band together to figure out how we can outperform the other guys. If we win a free lunch for having the lowest wrap times, we don't let the other teams forget it.

—Patrick

I'll get fifty e-mails the day we post a new bracket of teams. It's just smack talk—how one team is going to wax the other—but all the enthusiasm that's released is directly related to work statistics. So they're getting bragging rights out of the deal, and I'm getting a significant rise in performance levels. And it's not management that makes these head-to-head competitions fun. We just lay out the programs and the patient-experience advocates make their own fun.

—Lindy

Contests and events provide opportunities for patient-experience advocates to work together. The teams are competitive to start with, and the extra edge really gets them going and makes the work environment even more fun. It's also visible, concrete proof that management wants them to be happy.

—Greg

ROF: Return on Fun

The ROI on the fun component of our culture is substantial: a stable workforce with minimal attrition. In other call center environments where we've worked, the *goal* for turnover was 100 percent. Here, attrition is just over 20 percent. We don't have to continually hire and churn through people, and this cuts our recruiting and training costs significantly.

Some cynical old-school managers and coworkers have a standard objection to any proposed culture evolution: they're too busy doing "real work" to waste time on a bunch of warm and fuzzy "Kumbaya"-style crap that reflects a naively optimistic view of human nature. Well, killjoys, listen up: evolving a culture *is* real work. And to change a culture, old-school leaders typically must first turn all required actions into scheduled tasks. You have to put a meeting reminder in your calendar for July 27 that says, "Go say happy birthday to Ann Weinberg in accounting." On the same day every month, make this notation: "Write personal note cards to recognize employee anniversaries and birthdays." If your company has an all-day cultural event like our Gong Show, your leaders simply have to put their immediate tasks aside to make the day fun for the frontline employees.

If your organization decides to kick off a culture campaign, responsible parties need to be briefed on how to work tasks like these into the same schedule format they've always been used to. If they work hard at this dimension of the program, all the tasks will eventually become habitual and embedded in their leadership style. Until that happens, many days of a manager's calendar should contain blended agenda items where congratulating an employee on the birth of a child shares space with a strategy meeting. Until you get the hang of it, it's got to be process-driven.

Once your company makes a commitment to evolving its culture, this game-changing step will inevitably make some modest demands on you. Leading by example is especially important in cultural efforts. We expect our managers and team leaders to recognize their people, but we've learned in other settings that you can't really say, "Hey, everybody! Make sure you walk around and say good morning every day! And don't forget to compliment people when they do a good job!" Your culture will only really start to evolve when your peers begin to emulate your constant efforts to reach out to employees and be approachable. Sadly, we tend to forget how great a thrill it is for an individual when a VP—or higher—comes up to his or her desk and specifically recognizes a personal accomplishment. You can light up people with joy by sharing some positive feedback, and it doesn't cost a cent.

The good news here is that it won't take long for your peers to notice the enthusiastic reaction among coworkers and the resultant improvement in attitudes. Be patient with managers who take a while to catch on. Kindness is simply not embedded in certain personalities, and it might take them a while to learn that treating people the way they want to be treated is still the golden rule for any evolved culture. We don't have egos at Beryl. People with egos, at any level, don't make it.

I have to make sure that team leads who don't acknowledge things like birthdays every day start to do it, even if that means writing them all down. I use a spreadsheet to make sure I don't miss any birthdays, anniversaries, or other significant dates.

—Greg

Focus on your people. They're the ones who keep your business thriving, and keeping them happy creates loyalty and commitment. If you listen to their ideas and regularly engage them in the company's thought processes and decisions, they'll stay engaged when the organization has to move in a different direction. And if you've created a reserve of trust with transparency and proactive communication, potentially chaotic changes can be orchestrated seamlessly. You can tell your company to cut expenses and fear no dissent. Everybody will be onboard immediately because they already have a feel for the financials. When they are treated as equals, they're glad to be part of the process.

> *I just came from a call center conference where I talked about how we go over financials with everybody in our town hall meetings. People in the room looked at me like I was insane. "You do what? You go over every quarter?! What if you're not meeting your goals?" Well, then we're not meeting them! And we talk about it. And we talk about what we're going to have to do to be successful. Whether you're a brand-new entrepreneur or a battle-tested CEO, employee engagement means communicating the truth and—much more importantly—listening. Ultimately it's not that hard, but you'll never get it if you don't have the right people. And if certain employees don't engage and don't find value in it, they're not where they need to be.*
>
> *—Lindy*

Fun in the Pressure Cooker

It's all about relationships. The twenty-five people in the account services department are the critical link between the company and our valued healthcare clients. A relationship of any kind requires communication, listening, commitment, understanding, action, and follow-through by both parties. As is the case universally, the customer service effort never stops, and sometimes we're managing difficult relationships. If a client forgets to tell us about an event they're planning, confusion ripples through the call center. And like every company, we sometimes drop balls on our end, as well.

Our job is to constantly resell our hospital clients on their decision to work with Beryl. Every action and communication we make has to support the brand, and this really does require an elevated level of consistency and commitment. As in all relationships, there are good days and bad. We have days where everyone is so stressed out it's easy for someone to think, *Wow, hide all sharp objects!* To get the work done, we're always looking for ways to keep people excited and focused on our clients.

Here's our biggest challenge in a fast-paced organization with many moving parts: How do we make sure everybody knows exactly what's going on at any given point on behalf of our clients? Determining the best way to show other departments and teams the "why" behind their value and the client's perception is important. It's a mission that can literally make or break the company. Clients watch every dollar, and on any given day it can take a great deal to keep them confident that *everyone* at Beryl is committed to providing service in the most exceptional way.

Over the last four years, we've done a lot of things to start fostering and building up a sense of teamwork within the department and with other departments. Primarily, we've focused on three areas: studying the way we hire, welcome, and motivate our own team members; educating other departments on our team and our clients about the critical roles they each play; and recognizing other teams in order to create goodwill and stronger internal relationships.

When I took charge four years ago, our team didn't have the visibility or the credibility we needed with some key departments, and when we had to go to bat for clients we were hitting communication barriers. People—many layers of them—did not know what account services did every day on the job. They did not realize what it takes to support clients, and they did not understand what the client relationship means to the company and, ultimately, to their paychecks. So before we could effectively manage relationships with our customers, we needed to grow relationships internally. The first thing we did was use fun and events to tear down walls and educate people about what we do. But before you try to use fun as diplomacy, you have to know how to use fun to build teams.

—Melissa Bloom

Building Teams One Key Person at a Time

When someone comes in to interview we do the normal HR component, but we also speak at length about what the culture part means and how vital participation is to our department. We've seen individuals who just can't function here, so we're picky about the culture fit—which in our department is not just about wearing pajamas on Pajama Day. It's primarily a strategic outreach to other departments to make sure they know what we're doing and that we appreciate everything they do.

Having the right people on a team is key. Thanks to hiring with an eye toward culture, we've only added highly motivated people. As a result, we've been able to make substantial improvements to the cohesiveness and effectiveness of our team. It's a team that recognizes that growing relationships is critical both internally and externally. It's also a team that has to think more globally about each respective department and cannot make plans in a silo or fail to participate fully in events and meetings. All departmental plans have to blend in with everything else that's happening in the company.

Mutual respect, sense of purpose, understanding roles, and common history are key building blocks of a solid team. Once the right members have been hired, we use culture tools like games and quizzes to break the ice, expedite bonding, and make new employees feel valued. For example, we'll arrange a lunch and play "two truths and a lie" with the whole department. All the members tell two truths and one lie about themselves, and the new hire has to guess which is which. New hires also take a department quiz that contains helpful questions about the company, resources they will eventually utilize, and humorous questions about fellow team members.

Both exercises are inexpensive, painless, and amusing ways for the new employee to glean a little background on coworkers and blend in with the team. They gain insights and knowledge about history that enable them to bond and contribute immediately. Other helpful tools that promote the same cohesiveness are the "Welcome to Beryl" greeting we give each new member in the lobby and the presentation of a copy of "Beryl Alphabet Soup" to each newbie—an official guide to the company's various technical acronyms and other "Berylisms."

Once we implemented these features, as team morale and cohesiveness increased, so did our participation in company-wide events—which further boosted morale! Major company-wide events are great venues for team building because different members get a chance to contribute unique, creative ideas during the planning process, which we keep collaborative and fun. One memorable Fourth of July, members of the department dressed like Uncle Sam, Miss America, and the Statue of Liberty. We staged a parade inside the building and put little apple pies on every desk. For Halloween, we invented sixteen superhero characters with special strengths or skills related to operational realities like reports and the different ways we support products. The costumes were phenomenal, and we put up comic book–style posters all over the call center with "good versus evil" themes. Our department also had record-high participation and support of the company's outreach activities like the "Back to School" supply drive.

Good Stuff

To sustain our team-building success, we had to develop other inexpensive ways to stay connected in a positive and effective manner. Stress also had to be addressed. Everyone experiences stress both personally and professionally. As much fun as we have at work, there are days we need to support each other in a different way. The following efforts have definitely helped alleviate stress, connect the team, and boost morale.

Giving kudos and recognition was something we took for granted. Too often in the "busyness" of the day we failed to recognize each other. We decided to make a much bigger deal about recognizing and honoring each other through easy methods. First, we incorporated "Kudos and Recognition" on every agenda for our biweekly team meetings. The first five to ten minutes are consistently devoted to this item. Second, we decided some positive behaviors and actions are too important to wait for recognition. So we pull the team together for a quick five- or ten-minute stand-up meeting in the front of the department to recognize each other in a public manner. This is also a great time to read any Beryl PRIDE certificates out loud versus just handing them to the recipients or placing them quietly on desks. This public recognition was well received and once again reinforced the right behaviors, attitudes, and our team spirit.

One of our greatest and simplest morale-boosting creations is our Laugh Box. Whenever somebody does or says something really funny, we write it down and put it in the box. We open the box on days when we might be stressing or having a rough time, pull out a few cards, and have a good chuckle. At every team meeting we discuss the Laugh Box or something funny that needs to go in it. Our Laugh Box actually "laughs" at you when you open it. You can't help but smile.

"Good Stuff Friday" is another tool developed to keep the team connected. (It's amazing how even in the same room, silos or communication breakdowns can occur.) It originated with a simple thought: "Let's try to end each week on a high note. We'll talk about some good things that happened at work, but it's also fair game to throw in personal stuff." Once management kicked this off, the team got behind it with a lot of enthusiasm on the last day of every week. One of us starts the e-mail chain with a feel-good update or recognition of another team member or department. There may be compliments to share or exciting news, like a breakthrough with a client. Someone may say, "Hey, my little girl Beth is finally potty-trained" or "Hell has frozen over: my boyfriend asked me to marry him!" In a furiously busy environment, Good Stuff Friday is a pleasant, friendly way to connect personally and professionally and to reinforce one another as equal members of a team. Some of the postings are really comical and end up in the Laugh Box.

One day it dawned on us that we were all using way too many Berylisms in our communications with clients. So we started a "Word of the Week" campaign both to spark an awareness among team members of their individual communication styles and vocabularies and to encourage more articulate ways of discussing results, initiatives, and campaign plans with clients. We tried to do it in a fun way to keep it from becoming one more tedious thing to have to think about. Each week we shared an example of good communication, introducing a new business buzzword and challenging team members to use it in a meaningful exchange with another department or client. We made flashcards featuring different words and held a contest with a prize for the most impressive application. The whole campaign was funny, effective, and very well received.

The fun, motivational "Dessert Ambassador" concept got started simply because one of our team members with a passion for sweets used to spend every spare minute talking about things like frugal cupcakes, cinnamon caramel flan, and decadent pralines. We like to tap into the different passions and strengths of coworkers for team-building purposes, so we finally just appointed our resident sweet-freak to her new semiofficial role as dessert ambassador. Why? To help us solve a common morale problem:

dread of meetings. Once a month, the ambassador kicks off a meeting by introducing a fabulous new treat. Trust us, people come to those meetings ready to participate. One day when the conference room was looking a lot like The Cheesecake Factory, Paul walked by and expressed some concern that this particular morale booster might not be perfectly in sync with the company's wellness program. So we now do fabulous *healthy* desserts (with an occasional Sprinkles cupcake sampler).

We have become masters of team building on the cheap. Bowling works wonders. One day, just for stress relief, we bought popcorn and snacks and went into the training room, divided into teams, and played the game Scene It? together. We'll do a potluck or grill out on the patio to celebrate a successful client conference, and we'll use the gathering to talk about what we discussed with the customers. One team member had an annual calendar with a different Jeopardy question for each day; she'd stand up every Friday and ask the five questions for that week out loud. It was essentially just a quick, ten-minute stress-reliever. We've also shaved fifteen minutes off a stagnant meeting to go outside and bounce a basketball around in hopes that fresh air would jumpstart a brainstorm.

It's not always easy, and we have to keep it to a minimum because of client demands, but all morale boosters are good stuff. They help us get through a lot of the ongoing challenges, and it's nice to see the team come together. Part of our initial challenge was making the team feel it was OK to take a break from their roles and be part of the culture at Beryl—to really embrace the uniqueness of the work environment. And surprisingly, this strategic use of fun events has actually made it cooler to *be* a part of the team than *not* be a part of the team. It's not peer pressure; people genuinely *want* to be in an innovative department that takes things to the next level when it comes to evangelizing the culture.

I worked for a corporate healthcare company for a long time, in a department that essentially had identical responsibilities. Here, we're taking the same basic function and being more creative with it. We make it a fun process to get the attention of employees and lift them up. I sure don't want it to sound like all fun and games, because we work incredibly hard.
—Melissa Barnes

Fun as Diplomacy

Account management represents the client and their needs internally, and we also educate others on the value Beryl needs to bring to our clients. We can't bring that value without everyone's hard work and dedication, but when coworkers see us coming with a look of urgency on our faces it's not unfair for them to think, *Oh, no! Here come the bad news bears again!* Our IT department, for example, is never thrilled by client requests for changes or enhancements to our existing reports and services. It's not that they don't care, but these modifications can turn their carefully planned world upside down at times. Clients always want *something*, so we're not always the favorites with other departments, either.

Basically, it's a right hand–left hand communications challenge. We know exactly what the clients are doing, and we have to find the best way to articulate the information so that other departments will get on board with the mission. This requires diplomacy, and fun events are just another way we reach out to recognize other teams and build durable relationships that ensure a smooth performance by the whole organization.

We've invited the entire IT department to specially prepared dinners to show our appreciation. (Spaghetti always seems to improve the rapport.) When we sense low morale or tension, we'll invite other departments to breakfast. Bacon and eggs aren't inherently fun, so we've taken a team-building breakfast to the extreme next level by creating a diner setting in the break room. Account services executives wore waitress and short-order-cook uniforms with nametags like "Mo," "Flo," and "Joe." For an added touch of lunacy, we wrote clever new lyrics to pop tunes that effectively turned them into brand songs, and we sang the songs while people ate. It sounds silly, but the net result was more good interdepartmental chemistry.

Within the confines of our budget, senior leadership allows us to reach out and show appreciation to different departments in a number of creative ways. They know it helps the company stay solution-focused on our clients, and they know there's usually a sound operational reason for almost every fun thing we do.

We also started partnering with key members of other departments company-wide. To foster these strong collaborative relationships, we'd regularly invite them to our team meetings, to lunch, or out for drinks after work. Learning where everybody is coming from gives you a better understanding of what can be done more effectively. It also gives you an honest consensus, without which you can never build the foundations necessary to do great things together for clients.

Nobody writes more recognition certificates for the right reasons than the people in our department. We want to share information about customer satisfaction and make sure coworkers know why they're important to our clients. Beyond just giving birthday kudos to our team, our department gives every other employee a birthday card. We've been doing that for years now and it has fostered useful new friendships.

We wanted one new-hire class to feel appreciated, so we held a big tailgate party in our area and shared "Words of Wisdom" with them. We always try to figure out ways to include the patient-experience advocates. We came up with a quiz about Mardi Gras and went out to throw beads in a parade so we could meet with them and give them different kinds of information. Knowing the advocates usually have to stay on the phones, we designed a creative activity book they could peruse at their desks when time allowed. The whole thing was about what we do and why it matters.

—Melissa Barnes

Honestly, we spend a lot of time together, and how we choose to act or react can have a ripple effect—positive or negative. And if we're "all doom and gloom," that's reflected in how we interact with others. Our goal in account services is, "Let's make sure attitudes are what they need to be. Let's look at every problem as a solution." There are days when we struggle to find the right long-term solution for clients, but working on our relationships with other departments has helped tremendously. We have so many talented people throughout this company, and it's extremely effective and rewarding when we get in a room and collaboratively discuss solutions together. Over the past four years, I've personally experienced what it's like to be a part of a client-focused, cross-departmental team, and it is amazing!

—Melissa Bloom

High-Impact Recognition

A recognition certificate is a great way to motivate a coworker, but a well-designed and fun event can make a more profound impact. Our department carefully leveraged the company's recent Amazing Race competition to recognize our advocates and pay tribute to their contributions.

The entire company had the opportunity to form teams of four that represented our hospital customers. The teams made detailed models of these hospitals and talked about the communities they serve, so we brought the advocates into our area to show them how we support the customers. We put together signs, cute decorations, and food that represented the home cities of the five hospital finalists: cheesecake for New York, salsa for Miami, Chex Mix for Las Vegas, etc.

To demonstrate to the patient-experience advocates exactly how we quantify the value of the services they provide to our customers, we went step-by-step through the process and explained report formats in detail. This was invaluable news to many advocates who spent their whole day taking calls and collecting demographics but never really understood how or why the customers used the data. By helping them connect the dots, we sent them away with a heightened awareness of their role in the company and the importance of their daily efforts. This made them feel great! We even arranged to let several advocates speak to clients directly, an exciting taste of managerial activity for them. The cheesecake and salsa were great, but the heightened sense of unity is still in action.

Customer Retention

One final, major operational benefit of a fun culture deserves attention: it helps account for our client retention rate. We don't run the program to intrigue customers, but the energy here is infectious; clients are always asking us to send them pictures of our latest events. They want to know what fun event or dress-up day is coming up so that they plan their visit accordingly.

In this spirit, we try to use creativity to make them feel involved. A great guy named Pedro, who managed one of our major accounts on the client side, came to visit our facility in Texas. Twenty-five of us gathered in the department, and when we turned around simultaneously to greet him, he saw we were all wearing "Vote for Pedro" T-shirts like the ones in the movie *Napoleon Dynamite*. He got the biggest kick out of that! Another client who came to visit was born on Valentine's Day. We decorated everything in pink and red and put up a big banner that said "Happy Birthday, Robin!" When she arrived we gave her a tiara and dozens of coworkers came by to wish her well. People don't forget things like that, and because we do them often it doesn't come across as hokey or contrived.

Clients who come to Beryl comment on the energy and atmosphere—they want to be a part of it. It's about relationships; we apply our family approach to business to the way we support clients. Sharing the culture is a natural extension of that approach. It really is as simple as being consistent, committed, trustworthy, collaborative, and genuine with your clients.

—Melissa Bloom

Tips and Tools

1. **Carefully coordinate the culture calendar with department managers.**
   - Who does the culture director need to talk to?
   - What are the optimal times, days, months that allow maximum participation and minimal disruption of operations?
   - Meet with department leaders to coordinate events and implement learning or strategic objectives.

2. **Structure departmental events around performance.**
   - Start with bimonthly contests.
   - Give them a theme and let them run with it.
   - Target specific performance metrics whenever possible.
   - Regular "temperature-taking" meetings help determine urgent targets.
   - Give junior leaders the option to design and implement their own events.
   - Make sure incentives drive performance.
   - Incentives don't have to be monetary.

3. **Determine an ideal Return on Fun (ROF) measurement.**
   - Meet with managers to quantify the importance of morale to productivity.
   - Put together a trial budget that guarantees some ROF.
     a. Can you afford eight dollars per month per employee?
   - Measure the ongoing impact on performance and turnover rates.

4. Prepare your managers to make culture a task.
   - Expect them to embrace and implement the golden rule.
   - Make recognition an integral part of daily schedules.
   - Lead by example.
   - Be patient with slow adopters.

5. Make fun a key part of team building.
   - Brief new hires on the role of culture in team cohesion and effectiveness.
   - Use games and quizzes to help new hires assimilate.
   - Scope departmental events to rally the team and complement company-wide activities.
   - Come up with innovative morale boosters like the following examples:
     a. Laugh Box
     b. Good Stuff Friday
     c. Dessert ambassador
     d. Bowling
     e. Board games
     f. Potlucks

6. Use recognition and fun to advance interdepartmental diplomacy.
   - Cook for any team you're having trouble with.
   - Hold a tailgate party.
   - Praise coworkers through formal recognition channels.
   - Send birthday cards.
   - Celebrate the contributions of another department during a company-wide event.

7. Involving receptive customers in the fun strengthens the client bond.
   - Wear personalized T-shirts to welcome guests.
   - Celebrate important life events with gifts.
   - Implement client initiatives or branding into contests.

6

Caring and Recognition

By Jennifer Limon, Lara Morrow, LaToya Robinson, and Lance Shipp

This is the part of the business I'm most proud of. When people ask me if you can institutionalize a culture, I respond that you absolutely can. Lance and Lara are joined in this chapter by two people who are integral parts of our caring program. Jennifer is an HR manager who practically grew up at Beryl and is an example of how a smart and passionate person can grow in an organization. LaToya heads up the Beryl Cares Committee of the Better Beryl Bureau and never fails to uncover stories of personal hardship and achievement that we can recognize. Caring about your employees in the totality of their lives must be genuine. You need a system to make sure you don't miss anyone. This chapter will tell you how.

—Paul

When management teams become aware of problematic HR situations, they tend not to share or act on the information because they're afraid of violating privacy issues. We break quite a few HR policies to do the right thing and to embrace employees in need. Beryl Cares is an innovative program designed to help coworkers, each one of whom we consider a member of the Beryl family. The program incorporates everything from the flowers we send hospitalized employees to covering months of salary for coworkers who need emergency leave for critical reasons.

We also have a strong recognition program, PRIDE@Beryl, which celebrates the good things happening in the lives of employees. The PRIDE program enforces our strong commitment to morale, and we offer details in the second half of this chapter.

Making the Call

Beryl Cares began informally, with Paul, Lance, and Lara reviewing exceptional HR cases on a one-by-one basis as they popped up. When one advocate got word that his mother was dying of cancer, for example, we bought him a plane ticket home and continued to pay him for four months while he helped her through her final days. When a female coworker needed to move away from a violent boyfriend, we bought bedding and basic kitchen supplies for her new apartment and put her in touch with an organization that helps abused women. Over the years, Beryl Cares has dealt with hundreds of such unusual situations. As the program evolved and expanded, we put more formal structure around the implementation.

The process typically starts with someone approaching the culture exec and saying, "You know Ann in account services? Well, her apartment was broken into last night and the thieves took *everything*. They even stole all the clothes for her new baby!" All employees know they're welcome to inform their managers about extraordinary personnel developments like these. The program became such an icon at Beryl that we formalized it with a link on the intranet for sending in Beryl Cares information to the culture exec and the Beryl Cares BBB Subcommittee leader.

I'm the subcommittee leader for Beryl Cares because I tend to be the person in the company who people go to when they find out someone has a difficult situation. An organization wanting to start a similar program would need a point person very much in tune with their employees so that person can filter the conversation and discuss the important information with the appropriate people.

—*LaToya*

The culture director or subcommittee leader will send an e-mail to Paul and Lance with a photo of the affected person, his or her home address, an explanation of the emergency, actions that have been taken, and suggested future actions. If an employee was suddenly hospitalized, the e-mail would include an update on the medical situation, the address of the facility, and perhaps a recommendation that the top senior executives make a hospital visit. Both have made many such trips. Immediately after receiving the e-mail, they each write a personal message on Beryl Cares stationery, which is mailed to the employee's home address.

The culture director has a general ledger budget and a Beryl Cares general ledger code. Each situation is different, so they are assessed individually. Beryl Cares is such a part of Beryl's culture that often the workers take charge and start a donation effort or food delivery schedule. In more serious cases, deciding what to do involves a number of discretionary factors. If it looks like we might need to keep paying someone while they have to be out, the culture director partners closely with HR's payroll team. There are so many details that can change a seemingly similar situation to ones with different outcomes. A coworker's tenure, performance, ability to produce appropriate records (funeral information, police reports, etc.), and their personal situation all make a difference in the decision of what action to take.

If there's a catastrophic accident, the manager of the employee immediately sends an e-mail to me and I start figuring out what needs to happen next. To balance that person's emergency against our business realities, I'll go to HR and ask questions like, "What kind of a performer is this person? How much vacation do they have?" If the employee is going to be in the hospital for three weeks and only has a week of sick time, we may give her two weeks of Beryl Cares and then reassess the case in three weeks.

We always try to put the needy party first, but if he's on a third written warning with a poor attendance record, we may not be quite so generous. And if the only data coordinator on a major account needs three weeks off to be with her sick sister, we may offer a creative way to allow the employee to spend time with her sister and still support business needs.

—Lara

Gimme! Gimme! Gimme?

One challenge to a program like Beryl Cares is the entitlement mentality that tends to flare up in progressive cultures. When some people hear about the company's charitable outreach to a truly needy employee, they're not shy about making less valid petitions on their own behalf. We've had more than a few employees who thought we should pay their salaries *and their bills.* One young woman asked us to cover the $500 deductible for hail damage to her car. Another asked us to pay to get her repossessed car out of the bank's clutches. We don't like to provide short-term solutions—to someone with a budgeting problem, for instance. Instead we like to help with a long-term solution. In credible instances, we may end up making the coworker a loan, directing them to an outside agency, or simply explaining the facts of life.

There are no manuals for how to determine these cases from an HR liability point of view, but the right thing to do is almost always cut-and-dried. It's easy to differentiate between humble people with serious emergency needs and opportunists who virtually demand assistance with personal problems of their own making. Still, the program manager must be able to make quick, unbiased assessments and trust her gut.

When a trainer recently told a promising new hire that her ripped jeans were inappropriate, the new hire confided with great embarrassment that those jeans were the most presentable clothing she owned. Without hesitation, our culture director went out and bought her several different new outfits, some jewelry, and even a little bit of lip gloss—all for the whopping sum of $104. When asked why she'd risked any money at all on a person who'd only been onboard two weeks, she said, "This one is different. I just feel it." The trainee with the torn pants has now been an exemplary contributor for three years and remains unusually dedicated to a culture that took a chance on her. Small investments like this make an *enormous* impact on people.

To say no in a nice way, the program manager needs a backbone and well-developed communication skills. Even though you may decline to help an individual monetarily, you can still make them feel helped—and deeply cared for—just by being there and listening. The program manager must also feel comfortable managing up and telling senior execs, "This employee is basically shaking us down; don't give him any money. Here's how to respond to this person." We still laugh about the childless employee who sent Paul an e-mail asking for money to help her get diapers for her baby. She didn't think he would find out that she had no children! In situations like this, you can rely on a good culture director to keep you informed.

And, again, over the years, we've basically seen that employees who are truly in need don't ask for help. They're usually ethical and determined to help themselves, and we usually find out about their situations from a coworker.

> *The image of a company's top leader is important and you don't want that tarnished. He or she may direct a needy employee somewhere else or give them sage advice, but the top leader should not be the person who says no in these types of situations. Saying no comes easy to me because I wear the financial hat, and Lara is trained in crucial conversations, so it's better that we be the ones to clean up the special HR situations.*
>
> *—Lance*

> *Whether we say no or yes, we have other places to refer people. It's important to be able to help them in-house, but you also need to have a carefully compiled list of additional resources like community centers, food banks, and other credible support agencies. These are all posted on our intranet.*
>
> *—Jennifer*

Privacy and Cost Issues

Even after helping hundreds of employees over the years, privacy concerns have never caused a legal problem. We always consult discreetly with a struggling coworker before we arrange a public effort on their behalf, and we only do so for critical situations like a house gutted by fire, a serious disease, or a bad car wreck. Financial problems and minor emergencies always stay confidential. We have been known to organize a bake sale on someone's behalf, and the company will match the proceeds. We never communicate anything to the organization without the express approval of the beneficiary. One cancer survivor politely declined at first when we asked if we could sponsor walkers in a fundraising event in her honor, but after considering the matter for a couple of days she took a liking to the idea.

With a little bit of tact and consideration, you can always protect a person's privacy and pride. Some of our advocates are single moms supporting children, and they do occasionally live paycheck to paycheck. If we learn that somebody is having a particularly hard time financially, the culture director may throw together a food basket and send them an e-mail saying, "There's a little prize for you under your desk." Or she'll call them up to her office and say, "Give me your keys and I'll take these groceries to your car." Coworkers don't think twice about it because we do regular contests for food baskets and other prizes.

> *Because of the entitlement mentality, we have to be careful about what we do publicly. Otherwise, people feel left out and you open yourself up to unjust accusations of favoritism from people who don't know the details of the situation. We leave it up to employees to coordinate things like baby showers and anniversary parties for one another because the company can't do that for everyone. So a lot of our employees arrange those events for one another, which makes the issue easier for us from a legal standpoint.*
>
> *—Jennifer*

It Pays to Care

While Beryl Cares began as and remains a purely charitable effort and was never deliberately intended to generate benefits for the company, it has created some intense loyalty, which is never a bad thing. A seven-year employee who has a one-year-old son suffered a stroke and spent four months in intensive care. He only had one week of vacation at the time, but he didn't miss a paycheck during those four months. Since he returned, his performance and loyalty remain. He is a part of the Beryl family and he knew he could count on his job being here while he took care of his own family. Employees who know that they are cared for simply give more to an organization. That's why the top priority in the company's Circle of Growth philosophy is fostering employee loyalty.

The Beryl Cares program helps reduce the turnover rate in an organization where the cost of training a single new patient-experience advocate is substantial. It also has a strong catalytic effect that's harder to measure. A supportive sensibility has spread out and taken hold throughout the organization, and it's now generally understood that taking care of one another is expected behavior. A department, of its own volition, will not hesitate to buy a restaurant gift card for a worker in another department who is having knee surgery and might not be able to cook for her family. There is no real set of rules and little debate when it comes to helping people. When you make compassion your number one hiring requirement, you end up with a company full of givers.

One advocate, a single mom, happened to lose $150 in cash. Her team got together and collected donations to replace the money so she would have gas and food until the next payday. The culture director and HR managers never knew about this. The only people who knew were the employee's team members, and they kept it to themselves. When another patient-experience advocate got sad news recently of a relative who had been murdered, her teammates immediately started collecting money to buy her a plane ticket home. Now that is family!

In the BBB we've been told to take it on ourselves to help people out, so when I see somebody going through a difficult time I know it's my duty to ask others, "Do you see that we need to help this person?" When somebody in my department had eye cancer, we all wanted to buy her an iPod so she could listen to music after her surgery. But we didn't go to HR and

say, "Can you approve it?" We just sent out e-mails, asked
for donations, and it happened. Beryl seems to always match
efforts like this.

—LaToya

A lot of the Beryl Cares program is simply caring enough to know what's going on in the lives of your people. If a patient-experience advocate who just had a baby is out for six weeks and is missing some income because she doesn't have short-term disability, our culture director will buy diapers, formula, and other useful items for newborns and stick it in the new mom's car. Probably 90 percent of the company's caring program consists of small gestures like this, and the human touch is every bit as valued in these instances as the big dramatic donations.

The six subcommittee leaders on the employee culture committee often arrange secret outreach efforts. They refer to these discreet charitable efforts as the "Beryl Angels" campaign. Most employees have never heard the term because the disbursers of the gifts never leave a note. They much prefer to remain anonymous while lifting up the day of somebody who deserves it.

Who deserves it? Again, it's just a feeling that hits me.
One advocate's husband left her with teenage kids for a
twenty-two-year-old girlfriend. She's stayed very positive and
productive through all this drama, and she comes in on her
days off to attend committee meetings and help with events.
She's just one of those people who always represents what
Beryl stands for. One day I saw her worn-out wallet, got
her a new one, and put it on her desk. We want people to be
rewarded for what they do and for what they give. So it's a
little bit recognition and a little bit Beryl Cares. It kind of
crosses over. Paul sets the tone with spontaneous gestures like
handing out iPods to all the advocates during a busy month.

He also gave fifty-dollar gas cards to the whole company when the price of gas was out of sight. That last gesture cost the company $17,000, but you can't put a price on the morale boost—and the loyalty—that gestures like that create.

—Lara

Take Pride in Your Employees

Caring is essentially an evolved form of recognition, and Beryl Cares is not just a calamity relief fund. There's a positive side that incorporates a lot of recognition. If somebody's getting married or a baby is being born, we buy a gift and add a Beryl Cares card that says, "Love, Your Beryl Family." For example, one of our patient-experience advocates who does brilliant puppet shows for kids in her spare time just won a trophy in a competition. Some companies might not consider that newsworthy, but we absolutely do because it's the most important thing in her world. To celebrate her achievement, we did a write-up in the Beryl Cares section of our employee magazine right alongside the stories about new babies and sons who won Little League championships. It reinforces the idea that this company has a strong family sensibility.

Beryl has been recognizing people from day one, but in 2002 we formalized a program called PRIDE: Peers Recognizing Individual Deeds of Excellence. We wanted a public forum where anyone could recognize anyone else, not just managers recognizing direct reports and peers recognizing one another. Anybody across the board can participate. An advocate can send a PRIDE certificate to the CEO or to someone in account management. Anyone can get on our intranet, click on the PRIDE logo, and complete a form that generates a delivered certificate. And it's not like, "Someone just gave me a Coke in the hall and smiled! Hooray! I'm giving them a PRIDE certificate!" They have to specify one of the five core values that their nominee represented while going above and beyond the call of their normal job: passion for customer service, always doing the right thing, never sacrificing quality, spirit of camaraderie, or commitment to accountability.

The culture director reviews all nominations. If there's something questionable, she can send the form back with helpful input: "This doesn't quite merit a PRIDE certificate; why don't you write the person a nice note instead?" For the first couple years we really had to kick them back and keep saying: "This isn't *over and above*; it falls within the scope of their job." You have to train people to understand the concept, but eventually they'll get it. Here's a legitimate PRIDE nomination:

> I wanted to let you know about the actions of one of the Beryl family members. I just found out that patient-experience advocate Jennifer Perkins had had an eye infection and was finally able to come back to work on Monday after missing a few days last week. It's a pretty serious infection that can cause lasting damage. Her coworker, Monica Martinez, didn't want her to feel uncomfortable when she returned to work wearing an eye patch. Monica went above and beyond for Jennifer by coming in fully dressed like a pirate. She went to Party City and got eye patches, earrings, and tattoos for everyone on her team. It turned out that she got other teams to participate as well. She was very successful in making sure that Jennifer felt comfortable. Way to go, Monica! This is the true spirit of camaraderie.

Every week, an assistant prints the approved PRIDE certificates on impressive card stock. These are attractively signed and given to the honorees' managers, who deliver them as they see fit. If the recipient likes public recognition, the manager can hand it out at a meeting. If the recipient is less outgoing, the manager might deliver the certificate in person with a brief congratulatory note.

During our quarterly town hall sessions, there's a drawing for each core value. We position five big jars at the front of the room and the name of everyone who got a PRIDE certificate for "always doing the right thing" will be put it in the appropriate jar. There's a $250 prize for each value. It's not cash, because the money might go to pay a utility bill and we want winners to end up with something special that they wouldn't typically buy for themselves. They tell the culture director what they want and as long as it doesn't cost more than $250 she gets it for them: GPS navigators, Wii systems, clothes, jewelry, and—quite literally—kitchen sinks. Most of the purchases are made online after the winning employees send the culture director a link to the product they want, but she has met people at carpet outlets and tire stores to purchase their prizes.

We also do a quarterly drawing for "Best Brand Story" and "PRIDE for Partners." The latter is a program that lets clients nominate a Beryl employee for a PRIDE certificate. PRIDE for Partners generates thirty or forty submissions a month. A nomination could be the result of a client's "mystery call" being handled brilliantly by an advocate, or it could be for an account executive or an IT team member who bent over backward to help a client. The fact that we get so many submissions proves that we've bridged a gap in our relationship with the client and become more of a strategic partner than a vendor. They interact with us a lot already and we make it easy for them to participate in the PRIDE for Partners program.

Other wrinkles keep the PRIDE program interesting and top-of-mind. Every month, we assign a coveted parking space for each of the five values. The COO and the culture director review all the nominations, looking for somebody who has truly gone over and above in performance and hasn't won a parking space before. The names of winners are sent out in an e-mail highlighting the details of their PRIDE certificate, along with their pictures. The facilities manager then puts their names under the value placard in the parking spot and they get to park there all month.

Our PRIDE program works because it's uniquely personalized, unlike other programs where you can earn corporate money and buy things online after a website response generator sends you a congratulatory e-mail. In a program like PRIDE, the personal touch is really felt. That being said, the personal touch does require manual effort. Our culture director deals with fifty to a hundred award certificates a month. When somebody does want a kitchen sink from Lowe's, it can take a while to figure out the logistics of getting that delivered. All told, the PRIDE program probably takes three or four hours a week.

Birthdays and Anniversaries

Every employee gets a personalized birthday card from the Recognition and Morale subcommittee of the BBB. The culture director keeps a spreadsheet of all employee birthdays and sends the R&M subcommittee a monthly e-mail of dates and names. They then choose cards and fill them out by hand: "Happy birthday from your Beryl family. Enjoy a Beryl Well Subway on us. Love, the BBB."

We include a Subway gift card in each envelope, which ties in with the healthy eating theme of our wellness program. It's only a five-dollar gift card, but judging from the thank-you e-mails we get all the time, people absolutely love it. As noted earlier, if teams or departments want to hold individual celebrations, that's up to the teams. Many do, and we usually have a lot of crazy decorations around here to personalize birthdays.

The program that recognizes employee anniversaries is managed by HR. For their first anniversary, employees get a pewter pin with the number one on it and an eight-by-ten-inch certificate. Each year that follows, HR passes out a new pin and another certificate. The pins are cute and people collect them; you may see eight pins on one coworker's badge necklace. For third, fifth, tenth, fifteenth, and twentieth anniversaries, everyone gets a gift card worth fifty dollars per year of service along with the pin and their certificate.

> *I do a monthly spreadsheet to send to Paul that includes everybody who has an anniversary that month. The spreadsheet also contains their home addresses and how many years they've been with us. And in the "Comments" column I put down everything I know about that person— if his dad passed away recently, what committees she serves on, anything great they may have done recently. Armed with this information, Paul can personalize the note cards that he mails to employees' homes for their anniversaries. Birthdays and anniversaries are also broadcast on Beryl TV.*
>
> *—Lara*

For example, the culture director may inform the CEO: "Randy Benson just graduated from Tarrant County College and his baby girl, Hannah, is now six months old, so he and his wife, Julie, are probably just recovering from being up all night." The note Paul then writes by hand and mails to the employee's home may read, "Dear Randy, congratulations on your recent diploma! Now that Hannah's six months old, I hope that you and Julie are finally getting a chance to catch up on your sleep. Happy anniversary! It's been great having you here, and thanks for serving on the Better Beryl Bureau."

He sends out around forty or fifty of these personalized cards a month in addition to ten to fifteen Beryl Cares cards. People are excited that the top officer knows so much about them.

Annual Award

The company's ultimate recognition is the Barry Spiegelman Spirit Award, given out each year at the Christmas party. It's a peer-nominated award in memory of a founder of the company who died young from brain cancer. Employees can nominate whomever they want by sending in an essay about a coworker they feel is worthy. Every November, the culture director sends out an explanatory e-mail:

> Despite the challenges Barry went through, he was always optimistic and courageous. His unbelievable spirit was contagious to everyone around him. Barry's legacy is living on in those at Beryl who continue to demonstrate the characteristics that made him such an inspiration to so many. At the 2011 holiday party we will be honoring another deserving recipient for continued demonstration of courage, tenacity, and optimism.
>
> We ask you to nominate a Beryl family member who has exhibited these characteristics throughout the year. The recipient need not have endured a life-threatening illness or injury; he or she may simply be someone who displays courage, tenacity, and optimism in all they do, while always putting others first. Please submit your nominations in essay format, describing why you are nominating this person with as much detail as possible. And please include examples.

Three senior executives review the essays and select a winner, who gets a plaque at the beginning of the party. There are only two recognition awards given out that night, so the audience is very focused. Last year's winner was a coworker who always manages to create a fun, encouraging, hardworking environment for her team while also struggling with adversity in her own life. It was a truly joyous occasion and a fitting recognition of this genuinely caring person. The other award is the Face of Beryl award. The nomination process is the same, but the criteria are for the person who best represents Beryl internally and externally.

If you'd like to initiate a recognition program that includes caring, don't worry about getting dragged into lots of situations that require discretionary decisions. The company enables Beryl Cares, but the program just kind of happens. At orientation we don't tell new hires to be on the lookout for needy coworkers who they can hook up through the program. The only thing we mention is the positive side: recognizing higher achievements.

Caring and recognition help tear down the formality of an organization and make it much more personal. You can start off with the handwritten card component just to let employees know that senior management is aware of them and thinking about them. On the most basic level, it really doesn't take much to set up the notification process. You can then build gradually on that basic foundation in terms of how much outreach you want to do.

—Lance

Tips and Tools

1. **Don't be afraid to embrace problematic HR situations.**
   - These are opportunities to make a big difference in employees' lives.
   - Properly handled, the legal considerations are negligible.
   - If you do the right thing in each situation, you can always justify your action.
   - Sometimes the right thing is not monetary.

2. **Formalize a case-by-case review process.**
   - Have employees route news of all potential cases through the culture director.
   - Weigh circumstances against HR data on employee performance.
   - Notify senior leaders of circumstances and recommended courses of action.
   - Charge any or all expenses to a special account in the general ledger.
   - Hard-and-fast rules shouldn't block special cases that cry out for a purely charitable response.

3. **Prepare for—and discourage—"entitlement mentality."**
   - Your caring, approachable program manager has to know when to put his or her foot down firmly but politely.
   - Direct employees with self-inflicted financial woes to qualified community agencies.
   - The organization's top leader should not be the person who says no.

4. **A little discretion can easily protect privacy issues.**
   - Consult with coworkers before arranging support.
   - Food baskets and other staples can be delivered anonymously.
   - Never disclose anything you wouldn't want disclosed about you.

5. **The costs of a caring program are eminently worthwhile.**
   - From flowers to salary support, the investments:
     a. Promote loyalty and solidarity
     b. Create a sense of group responsibility among coworkers
     c. Dramatically decrease turnover and training costs
   - You may need to designate a pool of donated vacation time.

6. **Recognition programs can't be too comprehensive.**
   - Celebrate all personal events in the company newsletter or magazine:
     a. Births
     b. Graduations
     c. Engagements
     d. Weddings
     e. Honors won by children
   - Tie a formal peer-nominated recognition program to company values.
   - Make sure the necessary criteria are met, or your awards will have no meaning.
   - Present certificates with a "cash" award attached. "Cash" is redeemable for gift cards.
   - Use monthly drawings for special parking spaces and quarterly drawings for more expensive prizes.

- Enable your clients to recognize your employees.
- Create a link on your intranet for employees to submit accomplishments, announcements, or concerns.

7. **Birthdays and anniversaries are important.**
   - Send personalized birthday cards with a five-dollar gift card.
   - Handwritten anniversary cards from top executives should specifically acknowledge life events and contributions.
   - This information can be supplied by the culture director.
   - Don't underestimate the appeal of anniversary pins and plaques.

8. **A special annual recognition award can have a lot of impact.**
   - Make it a peer-nominated, company-wide honor for key values.
   - Present it at a major annual event.
   - Nominations in essay format should be judged by senior leadership.

7

Community Outreach

By Tina Clay, Sandy Reyna, and LaToya Robinson

Beryl is a national company, and most of our business is done outside of the state in which we reside. But we realized early on that it was important to connect to our local community— not by giving money, but by getting our hands dirty. This is tough for a call center company because we make our money by being on the phones. Yet we won't hesitate to take people off the phone if it means helping others in need. The pride we get in serving others is immeasurable. LaToya is joined in this chapter by Tina Clay, part of our data management group, and Sandy Reyna, a sales analyst. Like many initiatives at Beryl, our community efforts are cross-functional, creating stronger and lasting bonds.

—Paul

Beryl hasn't always been a presence in the community. We've always had great relationships with our clients, but it took a while before we really started to invest a lot of time and effort into local outreach. Once that process started, we had to wrestle with basic questions: What's the best way to go about developing community relationships? Should there be a fixed strategy and a game plan written down, or could we handle the effort on a case-by-case basis?

Initially we opted to support a single different event or cause each quarter, thinking this would be a good way to spread the benefits throughout the community. It didn't take long to realize that jumping around was inefficient and that everybody would be better served if we chose a few causes that really resonated with our culture and supported them consistently. After years of fairly intensive involvement, we've developed a few guiding principles.

Diverse Options That Match Your Culture

If it takes a village to raise a child, you can't expect your community outreach to make a difference unless a decent percentage of employees participate. And it definitely takes a good variety of opportunities to appeal to different personality types. Our environmentally conscious coworkers love community beautification projects like cleaning up trash along roadways and in the city's green spaces. Our "people persons," on the other hand, do not enjoy picking up snake skins and car bumpers. They would much rather be visiting with senior citizens, so we arrange opportunities for them to take gift bags to nursing homes on Valentine's Day. As you select the organizations your company can effectively support long-term, remember that you want to be able to offer a spectrum of options to your coworkers year after year. There are always enough community needs to match the interests of the most diverse workforce.

Your top consideration should always be: "What is the personality of our company?" Our culture director has mentored us on how to assess whether a proposed activity or event matches the company's profile. Character-wise, we're generally very family-oriented. We do well with kids and we like to have fun. So as we shop around to see where we can contribute most meaningfully, we tend to focus on high-energy events that benefit families and children. It's a huge plus if our own family members are welcome to lend a hand. These aren't rigid criteria, but they certainly help us sort through the numerous charity opportunities available.

Since 80 percent of our patient-experience advocates are females, one exemplary fit has been the annual fashion show fundraiser for the Open Arms program for battered women. Beryl is a major sponsor of this event. We donate prizes for the raffle, show up in a big group to demonstrate our personal support, and always have a blast. And no, it is not inappropriate to have fun while combating a serious evil like domestic violence. If outreach events aren't enjoyable, participation suffers.

Another perfect culture fit for us has been a local carnival that makes sure financially strapped families get school supplies for their kids. Many of our patient-experience advocates are single moms who could definitely relate to this predicament at one time in their lives. We have fierce competitions between and within departments to see who can gather the most school supplies for these disadvantaged children. The end result is *tons* of donations. Each child gets a new backpack stuffed with supplies, and our employees volunteer in the game area where the kids can win some really nice prizes donated by local companies—dolls, skateboards, bikes.

Some perfect fits for outreach seem to come out of nowhere. During our internal Amazing Race contest, competing teams were challenged to identify a community organization as a potential beneficiary. Team members had to research these charities and then brief employees in order to encourage them to make donations. A member of the winning team had recently read the book *Same Kind of Different as Me,* a touching story about a homeless artist befriended by a volunteer at the Union Gospel Mission in Fort Worth, Texas. Several other people in the company had also read the book and were just as blown away by it. The Amazing Race team adopted this charity for their challenge, which led to more awareness about the book and the mission. The book became the next month's book club focus. Pretty soon the story had trickled through the organization. Several BBB members asked if we could do something to help the residents at the mission during the holidays. We called them up and before we knew it we were in charge of the gifts and Christmas party for fifty homeless children staying at the mission. It was an experience that we never forgot.

> *The generosity of Beryl employees never ceases to amaze me. We reached out to residents of the Union Gospel Mission in Fort Worth and had a Christmas party for the children at the shelter. Beryl employees donated toys, clothes, warm blankets, and used coats. We delivered multiple gifts and a stocking full of goodies to each child. Each mother received a blanket. While we were unloading and setting up for the party, the mothers' faces were filled with relief, the children's, pure joy. We shared cookies and other refreshments while getting to visit with some of the families. Their stories made me realize how many people out there are just one paycheck away from being in that same situation. That experience was the best Christmas gift I have ever received.*
>
> *—Tina*

A diverse array of talents and interests can be required to pull off a single event. One activity may have many different phases that meet different personal needs based on what people like to do and have time for. On the front end, for instance, you may need creative folks buying, arranging, and wrapping gifts. When it's time to actually go out and deliver the goods, you can turn to your more socially active coworkers. These individuals, as one of our staffers likes to say, tend to have "more time than kids."

Knowing What Your Limits Are

Once we made a commitment to community outreach, we learned the hard way that it's easy for busy people to spread themselves too thin in this arena. Everybody here has a demanding position, and after the workday our main responsibilities are to our own families and homes. Coordination of time commitments requires effort.

Events and committees should always have cochairpersons so that one can fill in for the other when schedule conflicts arise. Make sure there's more than one person covering *every* key responsibility. Everybody involved with community outreach has to budget time to make sure they're covering their responsibilities.

The other major concern is to know the company's financial limits and work carefully within those limits. Our employee community outreach committee presents ideas for discussion to see if they're doable or not. Basically, we decide on what we want to do, then try to figure out if it's feasible cost-wise and logistically. Ultimately, senior management has to give the final OK, and a few worthwhile projects may end up being too expensive to pass muster. But sometimes we've used creativity to whittle costs down. Rather than go out and buy gifts, for example, we've made them ourselves. We've sold hot dogs and popsicles to earn money. The operations team sold meals and earned almost $1,000 to buy backpacks for school kids.

Financially speaking, we have a budget set aside that ties together different aspects of culture and outreach. Management finds out what we want to do and what types of organizations we're interested in and then plans accordingly.

Some of the cost of the outreach effort is covered by employee donations.

—Sandy

When it comes to gathering donations for outreach work, keep things voluntary and open-ended. Don't say, "We're asking everybody to give five dollars," and don't distribute a limited list of gift suggestions. Sometimes specific suggestions help, but if you let people give what they feel in their heart, they often give more than you'd ask for.

—LaToya

An "Embedded" Task Force

Over the last few years, the community outreach subcommittee has assumed more responsibility for coordinating volunteer support. This is one reason why volunteer manpower is never an issue. In spite of the fact that everyone is inundated with work and personal obligations, it's almost bizarre how all the troops we need just seem to sign up in a single day, and suddenly we have everything covered. For one recent event, we had double the number of people we needed.

A lot of this interest has to do with our culture and the fact that we always have fun. The members of the community outreach subcommittee are exciting, enthusiastic people who know how to round up people and convince them. And it's not exactly a hard sell when they approach you and say, "Remember how much fun we had last year when we helped the homeless shelter? Well, we're doing it again!"

People see that the committee is doing things and having fun getting out in the community. They see that we're being recognized internally by management, too—not just as individuals, but also for being part of something bigger. The team of new hires that just started is already asking, "How do I get on the committee? How can I get more centrally involved?" Plus, we wear cool clothes! We've got these official-looking black jackets that make us look like we work for the FBI. But nobody minds getting dirty. Nobody minds having to stick around to tidy up after events. It's just part of the job.

—LaToya

It's only natural that the culture committee is driving community outreach, because our public charity work is a direct extension of the internal outreach and caring that makes the culture unique. We see many situations where management reaches out and responds charitably to employees going through personal tragedies, and that inspires us to pull together and help pull one another through tough times. The next logical step is to help people outside the company. It's cool to see how Paul's philosophy of giving kind of spreads around internally and then spills out into the community. When you've got goodwill coming at you all the time, you want to be able to give it to someone else. The culture incentivizes that attitude. It makes you want to be a better person.

It's touching to see a new employee get hired on and be excited to come to work every day because she's happy we're doing something so unique and positive. People are amazed that they can be part of a six-week contest where one of the main goals is to find a worthy charity and then raise funds for it. You, the employee, have to go out there and make the pitch to convince your fellow employees to donate. It was a big learning experience for me, and it helped a lot of people gain an appreciation for a lot of worthy causes.

—LaToya

Be a Dependable, Enthusiastic Partner

We develop close relationships with the organizations we serve. Their staff members are on a first-name basis with many of our employees, and they know they can call on us in a pinch for certain things. We tend to progress quickly from no familiarity at all to the point where they feel comfortable picking up the phone at the last minute and asking, "Hey, do you have some folks who can come over and help us with this party?" They know we're *always* going to show up, we're *always* going to be on time, and we're *always* going to have a bunch of volunteers.

You earn that reputation by overdelivering. Two weeks after we committed to Christmas donations for the Union Gospel Mission, the largest open area in our facility looked like a Salvation Army warehouse. The floor was covered with clothes arranged according to age groups, from newborns to eighteen years old. Everyone in the call center jumped on the challenge and a lot of people recruited friends and families. We had so many toys, shoes, and coats that it took forever to sort and organize the items. At five o'clock the next Wednesday evening, we left in a convoy of vehicles. We unloaded gifts for forty minutes, and the kids' faces seemed to say, "Wow, there's *more*?" Every child got at least five or six presents and a stocking.

We showed the same intensity of commitment when we volunteered for a 9/11 anniversary event in honor of first responders. All we were supposed to do was help clean up an old fire station in Dallas, but when we got there we couldn't believe that the people who protect us needed so many things to make their environment more comfortable. The kitchen was deteriorating, and the beds were on big iron frames with what seemed like pre-World War II mattresses. We scrubbed floors, washed walls, painted, and put in beautiful new landscaping. We bought new mattresses, towels, kitchen necessities, and a flat-screen TV, and we built an arbor for the barbecue area so that the firefighters could grill during rain. Our first responders had to be thinking, *Wow, these people went 500 percent over what was expected.* We've kept in touch with this fire station and are planning to go back for more updates.

We've watched our giving spirit catch on in our own neighborhood, where quite a few businesses have gotten pumped about what we're doing and want to be a part of it. With seven hundred people in the building for our last Halloween carnival, we got a visit from an educational charity that ended up asking us to sponsor the Kid's Corner activities at their first 5K fundraiser. They knew we'd earned a reputation for dependability with all the school supply carnivals, but it's still flattering when people trust you to take care of children.

> *When I first started working here years ago, people would ask me where I worked. When I said "Beryl," they'd say, "Oh, that big building over there? I always wondered what that was." Now when people hear the name it's like, "Wow, I hear that's a great place to work." Word is getting out because of the things that we're doing.*
>
> *—Sandy*

Do It for Love

Please reread Sandy's quote immediately above. Now, be advised: we do not do charity work because we think it's good PR. Quite a few companies do charity work precisely and exclusively for that reason, which doesn't necessarily lessen the value of the money and services they donate. But a selfish motivation can certainly cheat your employees out of the real joy of giving.

One of our corporate values is always doing the right thing, which could be the motto of our outreach efforts. The biggest impact we've had on our community is proving that some people honestly do care. We keep coming back year after year, and we don't just dump gifts off and wave good-bye. Staff members at the charities we support have seemed surprised on occasion that we actually like to spend time with the needy recipients. We hang out and talk to these people and treat them like human beings. The purpose of the exercise is not to stage a photo op for a press release, and it really never should be.

Tips and Tools

1. Offer employees an interesting variety of outreach opportunities.
   - Build a mixed schedule for your "greens," "people persons," and everybody else.

2. Carefully choose causes that are appropriate to your culture.
   - Screen opportunities based on your corporate personality profile.
   - Be sensitive to issues of gender, individual skills, and family participation.
   - Make sure causes are legitimate.

3. Know what your limits are and plan accordingly.
   - Always appoint cochairpersons for events and committees.
   - Experiment with creative cost cutting.
   - Be open-ended in terms of employee donations.

4. An outreach task force helps rally the troops.
   - It also helps "tell the story" and spread energy.
   - Reward task force members with distinctive T-shirts and jackets.
   - Make sure to recognize involved individuals.

5. Be a dependable and enthusiastic partner to *every* one of your charities.
   - Develop a reputation for consistent overdelivery.

6. Charity is charity—not PR.
   - Keep a principled focus on human results, not media coverage.

8

Leadership

By Lance Shipp and Rochelle Revel

Lance is a great person to talk about leadership. Actually, Beryl was Lance's first opportunity to be a COO. He was a CFO in his prior jobs, but I saw something unique about his management style, and he was a perfect complement to me. He realizes that as leaders, we are only as good as our own ability to learn, so he is always stretching his horizons. As a matter of fact, right now he is in the middle of a fifty-two-week leadership program, and he is bringing great knowledge back to the rest of us. In this chapter, he shares how we develop leaders and gives tips for the journey in your organization. You'll also hear from Rochelle, one of our long-standing patient-experience advocates.

—Paul

A variety of factors contribute to the success of any business. As a private company with no outside investors, for example, we're free to take a long-term approach and make decisions that aren't pressured by market demands. We manage our finances conservatively, and we're zealous about things like quality control, value quantification, and customer relations. In terms of leadership, I'd say the two most critical factors here have been employee engagement and careful development of a senior management team that believes in our principles.

The focus on employees is persistent. We better their lives in innovative ways to ensure that they will take the best possible care of clients. The result is an employee turnover rate that is a fraction of the industry average. This basic formula has allowed us to double revenues, reduce costs, and win a slew of "best place to work" awards. And thanks to a solid senior team, we can grow without losing sight of the company's fundamental core values and beliefs. The following methods and tactics offer a few insights into managing a company built on employee engagement.

Approachability and Open Doors

A lot of companies claim to have an open-door policy; it's one of those generic statements most management teams feel obligated to make. But how many really mean it and promote the policy? When Paul and I meet with every new-hire class, we tell them, "If you have any questions, come see us, call us, or e-mail us." Anybody can make an appointment to talk to us—anytime about anything—and we'll work to make ourselves available. Approachability is that important. Coworkers have to see us as the real human beings we are, with their best interests in mind and open to personal relationships with everyone.

Is this a hassle sometimes? Yes, it is. Do trivial matters occasionally muck up our day? Sure they do. But what we may think is trivial may be really important to someone else. And most people realize that if they're going to go in and talk to the chief operating officer or the chief executive, they had better not be crying wolf. Employees who take advantage of this right generally have legitimate—and interesting—reasons and concerns. And the policy does three things that make all the hassles worthwhile. It clearly takes the top executives off their pedestals. It proves that the company values fairness, dialogue, and the voice of every individual. And it promotes total transparency throughout the organization. Everybody plays in everybody else's sandbox a little bit around here, and everybody knows what's going on—who is performing and who isn't.

Our employee culture committee works hard to make sure new hires understand that there really are zero barriers to approachability, and this can seem threatening to managers who come here from companies where nobody talks to the boss's boss. It takes them awhile to realize that while we do listen to everybody, we never make snap judgments without consulting the manager involved. In fact, the first thing we usually ask the venting employee is, "Have you discussed this with your manager?" New managers eventually learn to trust us, and that trust factor is what holds the open environment together.

Listening

You can always tell employees what you think they want to hear, but if you take time to listen they will tell you what they really want to know. So we've built a number of mechanisms into the culture that funnel useful feedback to management. We don't act on every input, but employees know that we take all their advice and petitions to heart.

A regular program of small lunch meetings with employees has gone a long way to breaking down communication barriers. In our "Chat n' Chew" lunches, Paul, Lara, and I will sit down and have a meal onsite with a whole department. We listen to what the group has to say about what's affecting them in the business, and we hear from the horse's mouth what they're looking for in terms of operational support. We always end the meeting with the same question: "What one thing would you change to make Beryl better?" *Everyone* has to give us an answer!

For a "Lunch with Lance and Lara," Lara and I go offsite with three or four coworkers at a time. The culture director (Lara) arranges the lunches, and the guest list rotates across the company. One month we'll eat with patient-experience advocates; the next month it may be application developers, then a mixed group that doesn't work together in the same department. We go to Chili's or the local Mexican restaurant and the invitation is always low-key: "Let's go get a bite to eat and talk about whatever you want to talk about."

The employees appreciate the free meal, and because the setting is informal they're not afraid to ask pointed questions or share an idea or a pet peeve. When you sit with them like this, you can explain things in a friendly fashion. These lunches are a cheap price to pay for great information, and they prove that we really do listen.

I'm amazed at the number of things we change every year. Either we find that something's not going to work anymore, or we continue to get feedback from our coworkers about new things they're interested in and really want to try. There's this constant evolution to keep things fresh, and listening is what drives the reinvention process.

Follow-Through

Whenever we meet with employees we take notes. At company-wide sessions and casual lunches alike, the most important part of listening is their response. If nobody ever hears back, the meeting accomplishes nothing.

When we give updates on major issues at a town hall meeting, we'll have a list of concerns that employees raised during the last town hall. We stand up and say, "Here's the follow-up," and then we work through the list: "Last month, Angela raised the issue of flex-time schedules. We talked it over with workforce management, and this is what we can do about that." Or, if the answer is no: "This is why we can't do anything about that." We post the questions and answers on our intranet because it's important for people to be able to reference their coworkers' concerns. If they have similar questions but attended a different town hall session, they can check the record for our response.

Nine times out of ten, simply responding to the questions in this frank fashion satisfies employee curiosity and makes them feel respected as individuals. The perception is: "I work for a company that gives me a fair shake. The answer isn't always yes, but I do have a voice and I am heard."

Leaders who make use of listening and follow-through mechanisms are more credible than leaders who don't. Approachability, dialogue, and transparency are all linked, and the absence of any one reveals a chink in management's armor that starts to raise doubts and can eventually damage morale.

Being Visible

If you are a leader, people pay *amazingly* close attention to what you do and say. Someone stopped me in the hall not too long ago and asked me if I was OK. He said, "Usually, you're smiling, but today I can tell that you're really concentrating on something." When Paul or I walk out on the call center floor, people immediately notice our presence and watch where we go and who we talk to. New leaders need to pay special attention to this phenomenon. Frequently, they don't realize that this constant scrutiny means they are setting an example 24–7 whether they like it or not. Leaders who do understand the potential of their visibility can use it in a positive manner.

Visibility is so important I put up notes in my office and in Paul's that simply say "walk the floor." They remind us to get out of our office, hopefully at least once a day, and just walk around the facility so people can see that we're supporting them and reaching out to talk and build relationships. Last winter, I got solid proof of the impact visibility can have on morale. We had a bad ice day and the roads were extremely dangerous. Our VP of operations fought through weather that turned her forty-minute commute into a two-and-a-half-hour ordeal. When she finally walked through the door, all the patient-experience advocates who had worked overnight applauded and cheered. Her appearance and presence on that stormy day convinced them that we truly are all in this together.

Once a month, every executive goes out on the floor and monitors live calls with an advocate. We plug headsets into their consoles, listen while they handle calls, and see how they're using the tools and applications. Patient-experience advocates give us invaluable feedback on our technology development and customer relationships. The last time I monitored live calls, I got a chance to ask questions about a new software product: "Is this helping you do your job any better? Could it be improved?"

This is a visible way of making sure the frontline workers know that we care about their needs and want to support them effectively. When you sit with someone in his or her personal workspace for an hour, there's often time to chat between calls. You ask about the pictures of their kids and their vacation pictures, and afterward you can write a personal thank-you note explaining what you learned that day.

Visibility at our cultural events may occasionally require an executive to look foolish, but there's a reason for that. It proves that you're a real person, not some privileged character at the top of a caste system. All these appearances contribute to a leader's image, and it's important to show employees that we really do believe the things we say.

Addressing by Name

It's been roughly eighty years since Dale Carnegie pointed out that people appreciate the sound of their own names, and human psychology hasn't changed. A prior chapter explained how the Beryl Cares program keeps us up to speed on personal events in the lives of our coworkers. It's hard to remember the names of 300-plus employees, but the e-mail pictures sent to top management as part of Beryl Cares do help us identify individuals so we can use their names when we meet them face-to-face.

One advocate who was fairly new to the company had just become a father. Walking out to my car one night, I recognized him from the picture in the e-mail notification and said, "Hey, Preston, how's the new baby doing?" The next day he told his team leader, "I was *blown away*. I cannot believe they know who I am and what was going on." We see instance after instance where personal recognition like this makes a big connection and helps us validate the individual. It proves that we care about what's happening in the employees' lives. Using simple verbal recognition just a few times a week adds tremendous power to your visibility.

Senior Team

The team that gets you from A to B isn't always the one that gets you from B to C, and it takes courage to make changes and find new members. As the primary owner, Paul can effectively do whatever he wants, but one reason he's a successful entrepreneurial leader is his willingness to let experienced senior people run key areas. Our current senior team has grown to ten people and represents all the functional teams in the company.

The Strategic Leadership Team (SLT) meets at least every other week to talk about ongoing issues. In a company of our size, the senior managers have to have a lot of range and be able to roll up their sleeves and tackle day-to-day management. In a decision-making process, the senior team makes it a point to include only the essential members. Since some decisions may only really involve two people, the policy allows us to move quickly. The SLT also has quarterly onsite sessions and one annual offsite session where we work on one-year, three-year, and five-year plans.

The senior team in any company has to minimize confusion and keep lines of communication open because divisions in the leadership can put whole sections of the organization in disarray. Our SLT has disagreements and hard discussions, but we always walk out of the room speaking the same language—on everything from major objectives to the details of compensation plans. Unity is indispensable; it's rule number one. Having the trust to approach one another when something is wrong or you are upset with that person is key.

Strategic Business Group

Like a lot of companies, we use a modified "balanced scorecard" methodology as the tool to help us implement and track our strategy. It can take a couple of years to grasp the concept and to figure out how to use it, so we formed a larger group of people to be involved in shaping and implementing our strategy. This Strategic Business Group (SBG) has about forty members: the Strategic Leadership Team plus the next level of managers and coworkers responsible for key processes. The purpose of the SBG is to facilitate—and to force—a year-round dialogue about strategy. It's designed to focus on business issues and how they should drive and prioritize daily and weekly activities.

Most companies fail at strategy because they don't revisit it often. They do a once-a-year planning session, and then everybody falls back into their daily grind. You come in and suddenly you're fighting fires, and you can't get to things on your priority list. So our SBG pulls people together for a four-hour meeting five or six times a year. We sit down and ask, "How are we doing as a company against our objectives? What's going well, and what are the obstacles and challenges?" The meetings keep strategy at the forefront of everyone's thought process and help us focus on priorities. People have to report on the status of their individual objectives, so there's also an accountability factor.

Meetings conclude with an hour of open dialogue on a timely strategic topic. The subject could be customer support, benefits, or the best use of our resources. We let the SBG discuss and comment on any aspect of the operation that might have strategic implications, which really helps the people responsible for strategy rollouts understand where they're failing and what can be done about it. The focus and traction created by the SBG help explain why we're executing at better than 95 percent on our strategic items today.

Since many objectives require the efforts of multiple departments, the SBG meetings help people understand the importance of cross-functional team cooperation. Members of teams are frequently from different parts of the company, and this naturally breaks down silos.

Participation on strategy teams is especially educational for junior managers. An account manager on a team with an IT guy and a finance exec can finally see how his or her department fits into the big picture. If a senior leader asks the junior leader to get up and report on an objective, it helps hone presentation skills. This kind of mentoring and developmental effort helps junior managers get exposure to the rest of the organization and practice skills they will need to succeed at the next level.

Offsite Strategic Planning

 After the Strategic Leadership Team has three quarterly meetings independently, we invite the full Strategic Business Group to our annual offsite planning session.

We start this annual session with the combined forty-member strategic group. For a day or two, SLT members dialogue with and get input from key stakeholders and the people who actually do the work, while giving them more insight into the strategy. It's a concentrated effort, with each day involving ten-plus hours of strategy work. On the final day, after the majority of participants have left, the ten members of the SLT finish out the strategy.

Last year we went to a dude ranch a couple of hours from the city. At the end of the first night, we had a nice group dinner that gave folks a chance to mingle and talk. With the larger group, the facilitator will typically arrange a team-building exercise like a scavenger hunt. It's competitive fun, and there is a lot of functional team-blending because it underscores the nature of our strategy.

We always use a facilitator for the annual event. There's quite a bit of preplanning with Paul, myself, and the planner to articulate what we want the meeting to accomplish. The facilitator does a great job of getting us through the agenda and letting us roam a little in our discussions without losing focus. At the end of the session we might be pretty much brain-dead, but at the same time we've gotten a lot done and accomplished our objectives.

No Egos

We are always on the alert for oversized egos in our hiring process. Some candidates are obsessed with structure—where they will fit into the organization and who will report to them. Paul and I, on the other hand, have always been much more interested in the best way of getting things done. We don't really care about reporting relationships, and we don't make a practice of exalting one particular performer over everybody else. Similarly, we're not big blame-gamers. We know that everybody fumbles from time to time, and we don't decapitate people when they do. So we look for people with compatible personalities, and we steer clear of punishers and glory hounds. We remind people that we are willing to change anything—structure, positions, processes, etc.—if we think it will improve the business and not jeopardize our core values.

We've hired a few highly skilled execs whose egos definitely tanked their careers with us. Some of them couldn't deal with the fact that our open-door policy let their people jump them on the chain of command. As a consequence, we've probably had a little more drama in our SLT meetings than companies that are less transparent. That's an acceptable price to pay for making sure that communication really flows internally and everybody knows what's going on. This approach also makes it very hard for ego-driven people to work in a silo. Nobody can just go off and do their own thing in their own way on their own timeframe and budget.

Intensive interactivity comes with its own set of problems. Recently our product management group wanted to rush a proposal to a new customer. Technically, it's marketing's job to gather all the info and draft the document, and they usually do a great job of controlling a very accountable process. Marketing was buried with commitments at the time, so other players who wanted to help jumped in and began to draft the sections of the proposal that dealt with their areas of expertise. Their motives were good, but with all these extra spoons in the pot, people ended up stepping on one another's toes and getting angry.

And anger is fine as long as you don't let your ego shut down the dialogue. If you're perturbed, go talk to the person who stepped on your toes, tell them why you're angry, and then clear the air so we can all get past the tiff and move on down the road.

It's hard to find a great performer who can check his ego at the door. Sports analogies are sorely overworked, but they do apply to egos. The Steelers attributed their last Super Bowl victory to the chemistry they managed to maintain between superstars and other players working together for a common goal. The superstars blended into the team framework professionally, and our "no egos" policy tries to promote the exact same spirit.

Embracing the Culture

I know many people who work for American Airlines—pilots, flight attendants, and management personnel—and they all complain incessantly about the company. The attitude is reflected on flights and, frankly, it amazes me that American survives. We understand that any culture can become a self-fulfilling prophecy, so we bend over backward to invest heavily in employees who embrace our culture.

> *Senior management participates in events willingly. They don't seem to get embarrassed or get their feelings hurt, and we don't feel like we're going to get in trouble because we put Lance in a luau outfit on the wall. I don't know a lot of other places that would allow that. Everybody is free to be as creative as they want, and a lot of the fun is the diversity that emerges.*
>
> *—Rochelle*

When Paul and I talk with every new-hire class, we give some basic background on the company and our core values. We tell the new employees that we want to provide opportunities for each and every one of them, and that the people who do the best here take full advantage of these opportunities. And we're clear in explaining right from the beginning that Beryl is not for everybody. We say, "Hey, if you understand how we do things and you want to be a part of that, great; we welcome you onboard. And if you eventually decide that you don't want to be part of it, that's OK, too. There are lots of other places to work." It's not an intimidation tactic; it's a genuinely friendly reality check and a litmus test that we continue to use on an ongoing basis. In this regard, one of our client CEOs has an axiom we support wholeheartedly: "No complainers, losers, or whiners!"

Paul and I sit down once a year—more often if operational problems flare up—and evaluate individuals strictly in terms of whether they are positive or negative influences on the culture. We want employees who understand where we're going and want to help us get there, and we don't want people who just sit around and grumble about things they don't like. During a recent Beryl Institute conference, a guest in the audience voiced her frustration with an indifferent boss and a troublesome aspect of her job. One of our panelists gave her some advice I agreed with: "You have to learn to live with it, lobby it, or leave it."

We want employees to live with our culture contentedly, so we give them endless opportunities to lobby it. We're always asking what we're doing wrong and how we can improve the company. Most people have helpful suggestions and know how to voice them, but invariably there's a handful who would rather complain incessantly and poison the attitudes of their coworkers. We always give these folks fair warning. We sit them down and say, "Here's what we're seeing, and here's what the problems are." But if we can't turn them around, we move them out.

Last year, we had a negative situation with an entire group. The employees had all been here for a few years, and attitudes had soured to the point where they quit responding properly to customers inside and outside the company. They'd literally developed a bunker mentality where it was them against the world, and they were convinced the world would fall apart without them. It was painful and risky operationally to remove this cluster of workers, some of them in key technical positions. But post-op the whole company could feel the difference—like a breath of fresh air. The culture was no longer jeopardized and we moved forward leaps and bounds technically.

Accountability

It's up to leadership to build in accountability throughout an organization. A business student who did her master's thesis on Beryl concluded that our culture has an ideal mix of laissez-faire spirit, authoritarian elements, and team spirit. Really, you need all three to create a positive culture that insists on performance and accountability. It's tempting to pretend that there's a secret science to this, but we've basically just tried to systemize a solid "work hard, play hard" mentality.

From day one we tell employees, "This job is fun, but you have to work hard. We expect performance and accountability. It can get so intense at times that there will be bad days, but overall we enjoy ourselves." And we make accountability part of the fun. We make sure that people understand our expectations, we empower them to deliver, and we constantly share the positive results of their efforts and ideas with them.

In general, you get performance when managers communicate clear expectations and employees make a sincere effort to understand those expectations. It's an agreement between the two parties, not a finger-pointing exercise. Ideally, accountability should transcend hierarchy. We want every employee to feel empowered to be a leader when they see or experience something inconsistent with our values. We tell them to stand up and say, "This is wrong. This needs to be fixed." Part of accountability is incorporating that ethos into your job, making sure that you—and everybody around you—are always doing the right thing and living up to the company's ideals. It's something we preach and reward. One of my favorite quick reads is *Winning with Accountability* by Henry J. Evans. My favorite quick hits from the book summarize this chapter well:

- Hypocrisy exists in the space between language and action.
- When you're screwing up and nobody says anything to you anymore, it means they have given up on you.

- Nine-tenths of life's serious controversies come from misunderstanding.
- Without clear expectations, people are being paid to guess.
- There are no teams in ownership.
- The first great gift we can bestow on others is a good example.
- The "leader" in an organization is anyone who reverses the momentum of a negative interaction.
- Always operate from a place where your thoughts and feelings are in alignment with your desired outcomes and goals.

Peer-to-Peer Accountability

If the ten people on our Strategic Leadership Team can't honor the commitments we make amongst ourselves, how can we ever get anything done for the company? Peer-to-peer accountability is another major source of the trust that holds the company together. Without that trust, communication breaks down, silos form, and you start to see the backstabbing and politics that cripple so many organizations.

When you ask a coworker to make a commitment in a meeting, it's not acceptable to tell her you need something "as soon as possible." Be clear and specific about the expectation. Tell her you need it on Wednesday by four o'clock. This requirement and her commitment will be logged into the action-item summary and e-mailed to all participants after the meeting. Do we always hit these action-item deadlines? Of course not, but it's incumbent on the committed party to keep the dialogue open and the other person informed: "Hey, Josh, I'm not going to hit this deadline. Here's why, and here's what my status is."

It's a common observation that meetings tend to be all talk and no results. In spite of this awareness, busy people still get together every day, toss ideas around, and leave the room with no definitive outcomes or decisions. Time is too precious to waste like that, and a strictly enforced accountability mechanism can be an excellent productivity cop.

Subordinate to Manager

Too many managers are preoccupied with running their own group activities and therefore are unaware of perceptions they create among peers. Their mantra is, "Don't worry; *my* area is under control." More intuitive professionals put a lot of effort into "managing sideways" because they understand that their success depends in large part on peer relationships. Most surprising to me is the number of employees—especially younger people—who don't have a clue about managing up.

Your immediate supervisor is obviously the first person you need to keep happy. You have to meet his or her needs and make sure he or she understands what you're doing, where you're headed, and how you plan to get there. It's baffling to see someone neglect this relationship, and easy for me to tell when someone has the knack.

Once they learn that I hate surprises, they will quickly figure out which issues, both good and bad, I like to know about. My management style is pretty hands-off, so I'm usually only concerned with strategic updates, exceptions, emergencies, and what resources you need to succeed. Other than that, I want to get out of your way and let you do your job. A good up-manager can distinguish material concerns from trivia, knows how much room he or she has to run solo, and quickly figures out the best way to communicate. Is it "drive-by" updates—the quick conversations in the hall? A memo once a week? A phone call once a day?

I have to manage up carefully myself, because Paul gets uncomfortable if he doesn't have a clear idea of what's happening with certain areas of the company. I understand that his discomfort doesn't necessarily mean something is wrong. He just likes to know what's going on. So I make a deliberate effort to verbalize or use more formal notices in order to keep him informed: "Hey, you need to be aware of this," or "I want you to know this." Then he lets me do my job.

A person who manages up well is never uncertain about what is expected. If you're working on a project and you're not sure about your responsibilities, don't turn in something two days later that has to be redone. Go poke your head in the boss's office and say, "Hey, just to make sure I'm on track, would you take a quick look at this and tell me what you think?" Simple clarifications like that save vitally important time and effort, and checking in ahead of the curve is what open dialogue with a manager is all about. And the time to tell your manager you're going to miss your four o'clock Wednesday deadline is *not* on Wednesday at three o'clock. Explain and renegotiate on Monday morning.

Most people quit their jobs because they have a bad relationship with their manager. We use upward reviews to minimize turnover and make sure communication lines stay open. Everybody gets the opportunity to comment in a blind, anonymous manner on how well—or poorly—they're being managed, and we require managers to address all valid concerns.

Objective Evaluations

Excessively subjective employee evaluations are a common problem. Is this worker a good person or a bad person? Is he really living our core virtue of camaraderie? Part of our "balanced scorecard" effort ensures that people are more objectively managed and given feedback on a clear set of measurable expectations; things that can be graded, if you will. My quantifiable measurements this year are as follows: we have to hit our profit targets, the morale scores on the employee opinion survey must exceed a certain number, and so must the cumulative score of the operating plans of the people who report to me. Without hard criteria like these, it's hard to treat everyone fairly.

Expectations for individuals cascade down directly from our corporate strategy. We say, "Here are the overall business objectives and then the departmental plans that support them, and here is your personal plan as far as how you support your department." Everyone gets input on their objective criteria. If you don't think something is fair you can speak up when we're building the plans.

Every objective expectation is clearly visible all the way down and carefully measured in the performance evaluations. At the executive level, your skills are measured on these quantifiable results, and if you can't hit your marks or properly negotiate acceptable alternatives, we find someone who can. The cultural qualities we're looking for, on the other hand, can't be graded objectively like this. Fit is pass–fail. Subjective matters are pass–fail. If you're not "upholding the core values" then you shouldn't be here. Period.

When I got here six years ago, we had a grading scale of one to five, and almost all the evaluations were fours and fives. The graph was a hockey stick. Well, sorry, everyone can't be a five. A five is a superstar, ready for promotion. The average employee should really be a three point five, which means they are successful in their job. If you're a two or less you are flirting with termination, and a four point five or a five is ready to move up.

Year by year we squeezed the subjectivity out of the equation, and last year's evaluations graph turned out almost as a perfect bell curve. There are very few twos and fives, and that's the way it should be: a lot of successful three-plusses doing a good job. Objective measurements helped us evolve from the hockey stick to the bell curve. This also forces managers to have real and objective conversations about what people do well and where they need to improve.

Tips and Tools

1. **Approachability and open doors foster employee engagement.**
   - Be available to everyone by appointment or e-mail.
   - Living this policy may be inconvenient at times, but it will prove that the organization values fairness and dialogue.
   - Communicate the policy to new hires in person and through ongoing input from your employee culture committee.
   - Don't avoid the "listening" lunches described in this chapter and chapter 4!
   - Take notes and follow through. It proves that you really do care.
   - "Walk the floor" regularly. Be visible, interact, and call people by name.
   - Sensitize junior managers to the importance of visibility and all these "personal touch" issues.

2. **Constantly cultivate your strategy.**
   - Employ a mechanism to make sure you revisit your strategic planning targets regularly.
   - Whatever method you use, make sure your daily operating activities and objectives are aligned to execute your strategic targets.
   - It is important that the people actually doing the work are also involved in planning the strategy. Most strategies fail due to poor execution.
   - Emphasize open dialogue and cross-functional team cooperation.
   - Use these occasions as training exercises for junior talent.
   - Annual offsite sessions are worth the expense.

3. **Police egos.**
   - Creative tension is good. You are hiring and paying people for their expertise.
   - Practice walking in the other person's shoes.
   - Be vigilant about addressing and defusing conflicts as soon as they surface.

4. **Know who's embracing your culture—and who isn't.**
   - Culture presents employees three basic options: embrace, lobby, or leave!
   - Explain this upfront in a nonthreatening way, and make sure you provide every employee with sincere and genuine channels for lobbying the culture.
   - Identify positive and negative influencers and act on them.
   - Don't hesitate to protect the culture from intransigent complainers.

5. **Make accountability part of the fun.**
   - Have managers communicate expectations clearly and specifically.
   - Emphasize the collaborative side of the relationship—not the adversarial.
   - If senior managers aren't accountable to one another, they can't expect others to follow.
   - Coach junior leaders on the basics and finer points of managing up.
   - Everybody has a right to an objective performance evaluation.

9

Branding

By Nancy Lecroy

I think it is important for every company to articulate messages that "elevate" the conversation beyond the services or products we provide. Our customers are really not buying products or services. They are doing business with us because we have built a relationship of trust. Our brand promise allows us to do that. I'd much rather talk to a prospect CEO about culture than how we can answer phones for his or her hospital. Nancy has done a great job helping Beryl define, communicate, and elevate its brand over the years. Like Beryl, you can be a leader in your industry by changing the conversation.

—Paul

We define our brand as the intersection of three things: what we do well, what our clients value, and what we can "own" in the market over time. The basic goal is differentiation. Why are we better than other contact centers? What exactly is it that we provide healthcare organizations that they can't get anywhere else?

A move toward brand discipline can be a transformative step for a small company, especially one that has been operating on a year-to-year basis without a tight business plan or a clear vision of what it wants to be when it grows up. Good brand work helps an organization focus on where it's going and aligns daily activities and perspectives with a long-term goal. Market leaders know that if they're not reinforcing their brand foundation it can tumble quickly. And regaining market share is much more costly than investing in a strong brand strategy while you've got momentum.

Before I came to Beryl, there were so many correct business elements in place that the company was already delivering a good brand experience on a daily basis. But we lacked strategic direction for growing the brand. We didn't have a definite set of brand tools in place to ensure that daily actions were leading to desired short- and long-term results. Around the time I was hired, the company had begun to put those pieces in place and make that direction clearer to employees: where we are going as a company and what clients expect from us.

Companies frequently try to create their own brand tools with little or no regard for their internal and external audiences. A management team that thinks they already know what their brand perception is can botch the exercise by focusing on the good news and ignoring the bad and the ugly. The truth isn't always what you want to hear, but you can't build out a decent plan without an accurate sense of brand perceptions. We used a reputable consultant to make sure we got well-designed surveys in the hands of clients and coworkers. Since feedback is the raw material for all subsequent recommendations, a serious effort in due diligence like this is the only way to go.

A brand isn't something that can be fashioned at the top and then effectively pushed down, so we set up a broadly representative brand team to work with the survey data. We had patient-experience advocates, people from account and product management, sales, marketing, our vice president of human resources, and other senior leaders. Paul was on the brand team, too, but he didn't lead it. This team met regularly to settle everything the organization needed in order to absorb and model the program: brand tools, personal responsibilities, critical success factors, and a launch strategy.

Brand Tools

Employees need useful tools to help them deliver on a company's brand promise, walking the talk in every action and communication at every level of the organization. The first brand tool we established is our strategic role: "helping clients connect with the healthcare consumer." This clear definition of what we do as an organization gives employees great macro context. Does everything we do—as individuals and as a team—help our clients grow their business? If we are in fact fulfilling our strategic role, a healthcare consumer will always think of a Beryl client first.

The second brand tool is our guiding principle: "compassionate, personal touch." Employees use this principle to determine how they act internally and externally with one another, with clients and partners, and in the community. This principle was actually a phrase that kept surfacing repeatedly in the client surveys: "Sure, you have a great product, but the thing that really stands out is the compassionate, personal touch that comes through when you take calls and deal with us." Clients are the ultimate judges, so this was the obvious choice to become the guiding principle. In essence, it had already led us to the success we'd achieved up to that point.

The third brand tool is the company's personality, which has eight descriptive traits: friendly, collaborative, reliable, results-oriented, innovative, trusted, passionate, and original. Each trait should be reflected in the experiences clients have with us and the interactions we have with one another. We expect to be treated with a friendly demeanor here, for example, and to bring innovative ideas to the table that deliver true results in terms of the work we do on behalf of clients. Personality traits are meaningless if they're not all put in action.

The fourth brand tool is the company's core values. Organizations often fail to integrate values into their brand, but they're extremely important. Ours include passion for customer service, always doing the right thing, never sacrificing quality, spirit of camaraderie, and commitment to accountability.

Brand Stories

The fifth tool—the brand story—deserves a little extra attention. Brand stories ensure that coworkers can communicate a company's special purpose and value. Sometimes it's just not that easy for people to talk about where they work, so we have a standard brand story that articulates the reality.

Stories also promote a personal perspective. We encourage people to share stories that illustrate how coworkers actually live the brand. An example: I see somebody clock out for the day and start to head home when a call comes in that requires her to stay another thirty minutes. She stays the additional time because she wants to make sure the client gets the data he needs. In this case, she's modeling our strategic role because caring enough to take that extra time ultimately helped that client connect with the healthcare consumer.

Employees submit brand stories on the intranet and explain specifically whether they speak to values, strategic role, brand personality, or guiding principle. We get a steady stream of submissions, and they're up on the website every day for all to see. Quarterly drawings from the submissions reward winners with nice prizes. This form of recognition builds camaraderie and ignites a lot of energy and enthusiasm, as well as encouraging folks to continually think about the brand and how to live it each day.

Brand stories can be a difficult concept for employees to grasp. Another example: "I had my Beryl shirt on at the supermarket and the cashier said, 'I have a friend who works there, too, and she loves it. That sounds like a cool place to work.'" Why is that a brand story? Because it shows that just being out in the community representing the company can excite a person to share positive things they've heard.

Program Integration

Planning and launching a brand campaign can eat up 50 percent of a marketing vice president's time, but a well-integrated program will eventually distribute the ongoing responsibilities. You never want to walk into a department and say, "Here's your list of brand tasks." Let peers put their own touches on the implementation to suit their specific functional roles and personalities. Close collaboration with HR is critical. How your company hires and retains people is as vital to the brand as any tools your team puts together.

Our team met monthly at first; now we use quarterly meetings to do a level-set. The representatives are the program's eyes and ears, and they provide great counsel: "We're not saying enough about x," and "We need to tweak z." Critical brand components have been embedded into our balanced scorecard, so we've got quarterly deliverables in that framework.

Make sure third-party resources like PR agencies and designers are in lockstep with your brand strategy. They're delivering messages through the media and collateral, and you've got to keep them perfectly consistent. In addition to the usual close monitoring of graphic standards, we vet every marketing piece that goes out to clients—and every PR drop that hits the wire—for brand consistency. Do these materials properly explain how we're helping clients connect with the healthcare consumer? Do they mention "compassionate personal touch" and talk about brand personality traits, like measuring results and ROI? Are stories included that demonstrate why we're the market leader?

A tight plan for growing a brand will not only integrate brand tools, but also every other business tool at the company's disposal. We leverage every asset we've got. The Beryl Institute has been a phenomenal brand support. The company set up the Institute to help us become a thought leader in the industry, and clients continue to see it as an invaluable source of market intelligence. Our annual conference likewise provides a popular and enjoyable affinity forum and a place to connect with like-minded professionals. And our website, which offers a virtual experience of the best we have to offer, has also been a powerful component of the brand.

Being the Face of Beryl

Plugging coworkers into the brand campaign is by far the most essential task, especially at a service company like ours where employees essentially are the product. I have been at larger organizations that focused their brand strategies so heavily externally that their employees simply couldn't deliver. This lack of program synchronization can be fatal.

Ultimately, brand tools are about accountability and responsibility. They encourage every employee to take a look in the mirror and ask, "Am I living up to the values and the brand principles? Am I a true steward of the brand, doing everything I can to help our clients with their business?" Hence our campaign slogan, "I am the face of Beryl," which we have turned into a mantra.

To recognize an exceptional brand ambassador, Paul and other managers will close an e-mail with, "You are the face of Beryl." And recipients react with genuine pride: "Wow! I really am doing everything I can to build the brand." We send this salute to each other individually and to whole teams that deserve special recognition, copying managers when appropriate.

As part of an immersion in brand training when we rolled out the program, everyone got a brand tool kit with a customized notepad. Each notepad had a mirror on the back with the slogan printed prominently as a reminder that the company expects each individual to reflect the brand and to make sure it continues to grow in value. Every new hire gets a brand tool briefing at orientation, and we make time for regular retraining and refreshers.

If you don't establish clear responsibilities for this kind of steady internal messaging, it won't get done. I'm the brand manager in addition to my role in marketing, but no one individual can drive all this through an organization. So we have consciously integrated branding into recognition, rewards, and communications. Since we launched, recognizing and rewarding performance that really models the brand has been a major focus. It's embedded in everything we do every day.

My responsibility is to make sure we're executing the plan and giving our coworkers new tools to keep the program fresh. A lot of the most interesting update ideas come from coworkers who are genuinely excited about the campaign. Some of them wear "Beryl-wear" every day because they have so much pride in the company. Seriously, we've got folks who paint the Beryl logo on their faces. This is one reason why peers at other companies say to me, "Wow, you've got such a great brand. How did you make it happen?"

The short answer: by having fun. Building our brand required focus and investments of time and money, but most importantly, it has to reflect the personality of the organization. Brand and culture are virtually synonymous here, and the culture is what makes the company great. We are excited to come to work every day and we enjoy what we do. When you create an atmosphere where people are rewarded with more than just a paycheck for a job well done, you end up with proud employees who want to be here and want to do the very best job they can. From a brand manager's point of view, I've just got to make sure they've got the right tools to do the right thing.

Leadership Support

A successful brand strategy requires enthusiastic leadership involvement and support. Keeping that enthusiasm alive can be a challenge, because it usually takes eighteen to thirty-six months to document a true improvement in brand performance. So a savvy marketing manager has to be up-front and unapologetic with management about the fact that brand work does not bear fruit overnight.

Be clear about the cost of brand work, too, and very clear in defining what you expect to get out of your initiative. Your company will reap what it sows. The more lofty your goals, the more money you're going to have to put toward them. As mentioned earlier, it takes time at the beginning to figure out where you're starting from—your brand baseline. The most costly piece will be the brand evaluation study; a valid one takes a good while, and again, it's essential to use a third party. We paid our consultant for some of the early focus groups, but saved money by executing the internal campaign ourselves.

Then you have to continue to survey and measure. We do annual employee and client satisfaction surveys with specific brand questions that help us measure how we're doing with both audiences. These surveys are time-consuming, but they're essential nonetheless. Marketing administers the customer surveys, and we work collaboratively with HR on the employee surveys.

An interesting closing note: Beryl is a $35 million company that does not advertise. This may not always be the case as we expand into new markets, but for many years a vibrant brand has earned us a lot of market share that competitors have tried unsuccessfully to whittle down. We draw the most significant results through word of mouth, and that comes through positive client experiences. A recent survey said that 97 percent of our clients would recommend us to colleagues or businesses. That speaks volumes to the power of the brand.

A good brand administrator cannot duck the responsibility of being an aggressive brand cop. If you see negative things or behaviors that are contrary to the brand, you have to call them out. It's just as important to identify and get rid of bad behavior as it is to recognize and build up good behavior.

Tips and Tools

1. Take a deliberate, systematic approach to brand discipline.
   - Conduct your brand evaluation with qualified guidance.
   - Send brand perception surveys to clients and employees.
   - Assemble a broadly representative brand team to review data.

2. The following brand tools help employees understand the program:
   - Strategic role
   - Guiding principle
   - Brand personality
   - Core values
   - Brand "stories"

3. Make brand stories a mainstay of your campaign.
   - Encourage regular submissions from employees.
   - Display these prominently on your intranet.
   - Provide recognition via quarterly drawings.
   - Offer a "Brand Tip of the Week" as part of internal education.

4. Careful integration is the key to success.
   - Foster close intradepartmental collaboration.
   - Plug third-party vendors and agencies into the process.
   - Put all collateral and media materials through "brand consistency" reviews.
   - Integrate all your corporate forums, research, website, and other business tools.

5. **Plug employees into the brand.**
   - Solicit their suggestions for motivational campaigns and slogans.
   - Distribute customized brand "tool kits" to everyone.
   - Include personalized recognition in e-mails.
   - Include brand education in new-hire training and refresher courses.

6. **Make leadership play.**
   - Give them clear, up-front assessments of all program costs and time commitments.
   - Create awareness of possible cost savings through internal execution and advertising synergies.
   - Measure brand awareness with annual employee and client satisfaction surveys.
   - Take immediate action against trends dangerous to the brand.

10

Challenges

By Lara Morrow and Lance Shipp

Running a business isn't easy. Having a great culture doesn't mean we don't have many of the same problems as other businesses; some are even magnified because of the culture we promote. But don't think that because we're compassionate that we don't deal with these issues head-on. Everyone needs some tough love now and then, and we don't hesitate to dish it out. Lara and Lance have done a great job creating this discipline and expectation at Beryl, and they'll show you how.

—Paul

While the benefits of progressive culture programs are indisputable, the road to the promised land is not free of obstacles. The following roster is by no means exhaustive, and some of these have been touched on briefly in previous chapters. Our intention is simply to give readers a heads-up on the most common challenges and headaches.

Profit Versus Culture

The biggest challenge is making the initial commitment. You don't have to spend a fortune to have a great culture, but a long-term program that will generate impressive results requires financial support. Events have hard costs, and soft costs can include the nonproductive time of participants and volunteers. It's a commitment you'll need to plan and budget for, and it can be scaled up or down in accordance with your objectives and fiscal realities.

Once you've realized that you don't have to choose between culture and profits, your second challenge may be the tempting illusory options presented to you by economic cycles. Why invest in culture during a downturn? In an employers' market, won't your turnover rate take care of itself because employees are afraid to lose their jobs? You could actually be selfish and say, "Look at what a great job market it is out there! Let's dump the bottom 20 percent of our performers and hire better people for the same money."

The question you should be asking is: "Are my people productive, or are they just *here*?" Think about it. Does fear of losing a job really motivate a person to give their all to a selfish, calculating employer? What happens to the income statement when the market revives and everybody abandons ship?

> *There's no doubt we could increase profitability by cutting our culture—for one year, maybe two. We could just say, "Gee, we're spending x on the program, and if we cut that it immediately falls to the bottom line." But over the long-term it would destroy our bottom line. Communication would shut down, turnover would spike, and we'd have thrown away everything it took twenty-five years to build. The simple fact is that companies on the "best places to work" roster outperform their peers in terms of profitability and market value.*
>
> *—Lance*

Understanding Open Culture

Some new managers can't understand transparent work environments. They can't understand why, when somebody on their team goes over their head to vent about them, this is not an immediate firing offense—or at least inevitable career suicide. It grieves them immensely that everybody on the Strategic Leadership Team might know what's going on in their department. Getting folks like these onboard with our management philosophy is a regular challenge.

It's helpful to define here what we mean by transparency, as opposed to open-door policy or a flat organization. Transparency means that we share information like financials, contract wins and losses, and strategy. The real challenge there is making sure that people value and understand what we're sharing with them. If we post our financials and only 1 percent of the people in the organization know how to read them, what's the point? The challenge in that case is not to promote transparency simply for the sake of saying you do it, but to teach and educate coworkers about the value of the information shared.

Contentious situations created when direct reports bypass the typical chain of command are logical fallout in a flat organization that lets people communicate at any level. We tolerate this because it allows us to solve issues that would otherwise get tabled. Whoever receives the input must always be supportive and make the coworker feel like they got their day in court. We don't immediately go berate the manager in question for doing something wrong. He or she has to make tough decisions every day, and it would be chaotic and demoralizing if direct reports had unchecked power to appeal any call they didn't like. And we never, under any circumstance, allow the manager to retaliate against the coworker.

We used to just give management candidates an anecdotal heads-up about the communication dynamics. After some nasty flare-ups with newly hired executives, we realized we owed candidates a more purposeful and deliberate briefing: "Let me tell you what the environment here is like—and the formal policies around this stuff."

> *It's definitely a challenge when an outraged manager lashes out at a direct report and makes him or her feel like a criminal for exercising communication rights. In the past, when senior leaders went back and retaliated, we had to readdress the fact that this is not the way it's handled and do damage control to the group involved. The retaliators aren't with us anymore.*
>
> *—Lara*

We've also found ourselves challenged at times by the sweeping scope of the original open-door policy. The underlying philosophy will always be correct, but certain impracticalities arise as we get bigger and add layers of management. For instance, patient-experience advocates with a beef don't always take it to the appropriate authority, i.e., the director of operations. Many go straight to Paul instead because ten years ago this was a surefire way to get things fixed. It's still a viable and open option, but the notion that "I may as well go to the top" isn't perfectly rational.

While we may need to sensitize coworkers to this fact, we'll do it in a way that leaves them convinced they can still talk to anybody without fear of politics. Because if fear prevails, no one says anything and important information gets smothered. We simply ask the employee to think through who they go to and why. Paul isn't the person to talk to when the toaster disappears from the break room!

Institutionalizing Accountability

How do you preserve your culture as you grow? We've made a commitment to our people to do that, but we still want to raise revenues, be efficient, and document those efficiencies. It's hard to build structure into a freewheeling culture without crushing it, and there's always pushback when you try to introduce visibility and accountability. When we developed new management reports to let us measure people in new ways, some individuals screamed bloody murder: "You're changing the culture! That's not the way we do things!" Paul's reaction was essentially, "Are you kidding me? We're just supposed to take everybody's word that they're doing their job?"

We're very proud of our culture's humane orientation, but we're a *business*. And a business needs accountability to be successful. So we're perpetually challenged to explain how great culture and accountability work together, and to make sure that employees—especially those who have been here a long time—don't feel threatened by change.

Why should anyone feel threatened because their managers can find out what they're doing? A responsible employee would welcome the visibility so she can get credit for things that weren't previously measured. That's the way we hope people will look at accountability measures, so when they throw up the culture flag in response it tends to raise a red flag for us.

Negative reactions to change can be overcome by education and sharing information. Don't make accountability a priority one month and then gradually abandon the crusade. Have the discipline to stick with it and be consistent in the way you communicate about why you're doing things. It's just a matter of keeping your eye on the ball.

It's a challenge we're facing right now with the team leads. Our director of operations has a new ability to process very granular reports on individual performance. When we try to use that technology to hold people accountable, the team leads keep saying, "These new processes are against our culture." But there's no contradiction at all; you can have a fun, compassionate culture that also embraces accountability.

—*Lance*

Drama

Most business cultures are cut-and-dried. There are things you talk about and things you don't talk about, and never the twain shall meet. But even these businesses operate in a world infatuated with celebrities and political gossip, a world full of people who love to talk about other people. And companies that strive to find and keep the right employees are even more inclined to fixate on people issues. Transparent cultures have vibrant grapevines, and managers who don't know where to draw the line can end up reacting to trivial matters. Sometimes it can feel like personal drama has eclipsed serious issues.

If your culture also has an active program to track events in your employees' personal lives, you will definitely end up learning about personal situations that can complicate business decisions. While we're talking about a marginal employee's performance, someone will say, "You know, her husband just got laid off." That fact may have nothing to do with the individual's performance or her negative effect on the business, but once it creeps into the conversation a compassionate organization is inclined to bend and accommodate—even when it shouldn't.

In an open organization, too, some people feel they can get decisions overturned if they make a ruckus. We expect a person to give his opinion during a performance review, and if he wants to talk to another manager about an issue that's his right. Once a decision is made, however, the discussion has ended and so has all official tolerance for malcontents. If leadership determines that we've made a mistake, we will change it. Those times are few, but we've done it.

To avoid drama, individual managers must find a balance between being involved with people issues and maintaining the disciplined distance they need to prioritize the issues of the day. Junior managers frequently struggle to learn how to discriminate between idle gossip and personal information that requires a response. Careful coaching from a senior leader can make a big difference.

Entitlement

This issue, introduced in chapter 6, deserves some final consideration. Let's say you set up a program like Beryl Cares. You financially help a long-term employee who's been a phenomenal performer at your company for many years. An employee who has been with you for three months hears about this charitable gesture and comes asking for grocery money. He has a spotty attendance record and loves showing off the new car he bought last month. How do you deal with his entitlement mentality?

We've mentioned that, in a nutshell, you need an impressively tactful program administrator—someone who can explain why the answer is "no" in a way that doesn't upset people or make them feel like they're being judged or discriminated against. In egregious situations, this person must also be able to put their foot down and be clear that that request was inappropriate. They might need to help the petitioner identify helpful improvements in budgeting or spending habits, or simply direct them to a community outreach program.

Centralized control is also essential, because you can't expect other managers to know what's appropriate or keep track of what the company has and hasn't done for different individuals. Beryl Cares is purposefully administered in a centralized fashion to ensure consistency and control entitlement. The administrator needs to have an overall knowledge of everybody's performance and their other qualifications for assistance. Otherwise, you can run into trouble with discrimination or favoritism.

Another way to curb outrageous expectations is by not going crazy with incentives—a noble mistake we have been guilty of many times. It got to a point where if we gave a winning team a $100 gift card as a prize one year, they'd expect $500 the next year. So we finally said, "You know what? We're going back to basics a little bit so people can get back to appreciating what they've already got." And as a result of patient educational efforts on the Beryl Cares front, we're slowly getting to where people understand the difference between reasonable and unreasonable requests.

> *It's a constant battle. When the cost of gas spiked last summer, we gave everybody a $50 gas card. This cost the company $17,000, but I heard some people say, "I have two cars; why don't I get two cards?" And I said, "Hey, that's the way it is, and if you don't want yours I can give it to somebody who really appreciates stuff like this." They change their minds pretty quickly when you give them a reality check.*
> *—Lara*

Diverse Generations

Beryl employees range in age from teens to late sixties, and they represent wildly diverse philosophies of work. A typical Millennial certainly sees the world through very different eyes than a workaholic yuppie Baby Boomer who might recall some of his parents' lectures on loyalty, duty, and sacrifice. Our older, more experienced cohort tends to see some logic in an employee making a solid initial effort to build a track record and establish himself. They tend to see their paycheck as sufficient recognition for a job well done, and—having worked at large impersonal corporations before—they appreciate our more idealistic culture. Boomers and

Gen Xers who come in at a director level or higher have also already outgrown the need to prove themselves and feed their egos. They usually just want to be part of a team that's making a difference.

At the other end of the spectrum, we love our techno-savvy Millennials. They're the future of Beryl and we're learning to rise to the challenge of their generational quirks. These quirks, after all, are more a function of nurture than nature. Millennials are less accustomed to waiting for things and more accustomed to constant reinforcement. Many have never worked elsewhere and assume that humane cultures are the norm. They don't understand why the company shouldn't provide all their needs, and this expectation can prompt them to wonder what we've done for them lately. Comfortable with change, they're often quick to head off to places where they think the grass is greener.

Every long-term business model needs to give this demographic careful thought, mentoring, and proper channels for their remarkable collaborative and multitasking skills. We have a self-focused young manager who wants to rise in the organization, for example, and we're trying to persuade him that he'll succeed a lot faster if he stops worrying about his own situation and starts helping his team members succeed. When structuring culture activities, the program manager has to be sensitive to age differences and make a conscious effort to learn how to communicate with this or that audience in its own language.

The Senior Team

Here's a slightly paradoxical—and extremely frustrating—challenge: most rapidly growing businesses can't teach their managers the executive skills they need to properly run a rapidly growing business. And what happens when the loyal troupers who got you from point A to point B can't get their heads around life at point B? You have to bring in outside talent, which threatens the loyal troupers and seems to repudiate your past practice of promoting talent from within.

We try to deal with this by teaching the whole organization about the benefits of outside talent. We explain how these more experienced new managers have a wealth of resources they can share with loyal troupers, and how these mentor relationships will help our veterans grow in ways we could not previously enable. And we remind them of all the loyal managers who failed in the past after we gamely gave them a chance and put them in positions we couldn't prepare them for. The best companies both promote from within and hire new talent when needed.

Another senior team challenge: due to our emphasis on finding right fits, our average time to hire is two or three times longer than in traditional organizations. This takes discipline because when you're looking to hire someone you usually needed them yesterday. Senior leaders who've identified a candidate will say, "I've known this guy for ten years and he's *fantastic*! Why can't I just hire him?" Well, sorry, we've all got to go through the process and get to know your old acquaintance really well. A fair amount of highly recommended candidates like these don't end up passing muster with the Strategic Leadership Team. Our long hiring process has also prevented other major hiring mistakes as candidates dropped their guard and revealed character flaws.

> *Finding outside talent that really fits what you're trying to do is difficult and definitely increases the search time. Potential new senior leaders have to be patient during this long hiring process, and we try to explain that up front. We tell them we're thorough and it takes a long time, but we wear some people out and lose a few qualified candidates as a result. But if they're truly committed they'll understand what we're doing and be willing to wait.*
>
> *—Lance*

Termination

There may be a compassionate, high-performing company out there that never has to fire people, but Beryl is not that unicorn. It might take us sixty to ninety days to terminate a person for something that would get him canned on the spot in more doctrinaire environments, but eventually justice prevails. We'll expedite the process in extreme cases—like the fellow caught red-handed breaking into a coworker's car. But our family values usually constrain us to stop and ask, "Has this person been communicated with? Has he been through corrective action or guidance or counseling? Have we given him a chance to recover and reform? Does he know his job is in jeopardy?"

Compassionate firing—there is such a thing—can demand as much patience as careful hiring. We've had flabbergasted executives say, "This guy is *hopeless*! Why can't I just let him go today?" Usually, the answer is, "Because that's the easy way out, and it's wrong on your part to try to avoid the necessary difficult conversations with your people. If you're having issues with someone, have the discipline to start addressing those issues as soon as possible. And if you think you need to make a change, have the discipline to sit down and document that pattern."

In a culture based on open communication, people also expect full disclosure on everything that happens, including terminations. If you don't give them every detail, they can assume you're hiding something. We'll occasionally let a person go and then hear inaccurate playbacks that highlight the terrible unfairness of the process. In the face of such wild speculation, you just need to go back and have the conversation: "Look, for obvious legal and privacy concerns, we can't really tell you why Jack isn't here anymore. Our policy is that a person has been coached, so the decision was no surprise to Jack. And you need to trust us when we tell you that he was well counseled and well taken care of." If you adhere to that communication practice consistently, people can usually figure things out pretty easily. As a result of these policies, we have a reputation internally for treating people fairly and doing the right thing.

The same transparent approach should apply in the case of layoffs. As soon as you know you're going to have to make a hard decision, communicate with the people who are going to be affected. Treat them like adults and give them all the information they're going to need. Recently, a couple of customers had serious cutbacks in their business, which also forced us to make some changes. Eligible coworkers were invited to apply for open positions, and the few we had to let go got good packages and counseling. Even if you have to let a large number of people go, the key is communicating in an open, honest way.

Jeff, Becky, and Chad

There's a final challenge associated with terminations: How can champions of a progressive culture keep their faith in the mission when people they reach out to betray them and the program? Below are two tales from our crypt.

"Jeff" lived and breathed Beryl and everyone adored him. He was on the employee culture committee and the events subcommittee, and he oversaw the haunted house every Halloween; he was a positive team player. When helping stuff packages for our last Christmas party, he saw what kind of tickets we were using as drink chits. Then he went to the party store and bought himself a big roll of the same color of tickets. On the night of the party, he got drunk and started passing out tickets to everybody like a Vegas high-roller. Caught and confronted, he solemnly blamed several innocent people. Jeff would probably still have his job if he hadn't compromised his integrity by throwing his peers under the bus, but our faith in human nature would still be rattled.

Horror story number two: "Becky" and "Chad" were also exemplary members of the employee culture committee—our elite group. One day, a few fellow committee members approached management and said, "Gosh, we sure hate to throw Becky and Chad under the bus, but they've been selling hydrocodone tablets for ten bucks a pop to anybody who wants to buy them." Sure enough, Becky and Chad had been taking orders over their work phones and using our computers to send out e-mail invoices for illegal prescription drugs. Their lightning-fast terminations left another very bad taste in our mouths.

In the face of ingratitude and downright criminality, a giving employer has to grit his teeth and continue to take the philosophical high road. Do good when you can because it is the right thing to do. For every one who breaks your heart, ninety-nine will do you proud.

Nonbelievers

Our final challenge is not inconsiderable: if you own, run, or help run a company right now you can probably already imagine a cynical faction in-house who will sneer at any progressive new culture initiatives you might like to try. Should they be free to opt out?

We have a few folks who still don't throw themselves wholeheartedly into every aspect of our program, and we don't harbor any grudges. Some people come here from companies where all they ever did was grind, and it can be a difficult transition for someone that disciplined. It can take simple nonbelievers like these a full year's worth of events to comprehend that it really is OK for them to go outside for two hours and shoot water guns. Or to create train cars for our "start the kids on the right track" school supply drive. It's sort of like deprogramming someone who grew up in a cult!

But naysayers can take more entrenched stands. Some people say, "I don't know why we spend so much money on all this stupid culture stuff. I'd rather have it on my paycheck." In cases like that, it's helpful to work the math with them: "All right, we have 350 employees. If you want to split the culture budget up between 350 employees in 27 paychecks, you might see an extra two bucks every once in a while. But, frankly, we can't afford to cancel a program that's so integral to our margins and retention." It's also helpful to keep in mind that some of these people would be the first to complain if all the events and incentives suddenly grind to a halt.

There will be events that require different levels of individual participation, but for celebrations like Family Day all an employee really has to do is show up and eat free food and play games. Allowing ourselves to be totally unproductive two or three days a year increases the productivity for every other day we're working.

The best defense against whiners is to have a sufficient variety of events throughout the year to ensure that one or two things will appeal to all your different internal audiences. Last year, all our overly pragmatic guys who typically don't participate in anything else loved the "Balls of Fury" ping-pong tournament. They loved it so much they sent in an idea for a pool tournament next year. Make an effort to solicit and accommodate as many different ideas from your people as possible.

We had nasty comments at first from people who didn't understand the program, and every year in the employee opinion survey someone will say, "All this fun stuff is stupid! Why don't we just come in, work, and go home?" And Paul's mind-set is: "If you don't like it, go somewhere else." We're all busy, you know. Everybody's busy here, but we take the time to say, "The work will still be there in three hours—and that's OK." So it's just a matter of mind-set.

—Lara

Tips and Tools

1. ## Profit versus culture—think about it!
   - Convene a serious meeting and ask your senior leaders:
     a. Are we where we need to be morale-wise?
     b. How about approachability?
     c. What benefits might we realize through transparency?
     d. Would competitors and customers feel the difference?
   - Assess available financial resources.
   - Commit to the long haul.
   - Don't let market fluctuations sway your commitment.

2. ## School everyone on the benefits of a flat, open, and transparent culture.
   - If you share financials, teach people how to read them.
   - Senior managers should encourage and be receptive to all communication.
   - Don't yell at managers who've been leapfrogged, but don't allow retaliation.
   - Brief job candidates on communication policies.
   - Point individuals to the appropriate manager for appeals, but keep the CEO's door open!

3. ## Teach—and preach—the benefits of a benign accountability campaign.
   - Transparent reporting is a good thing for high performers.
   - Prove this by rewarding high performance.
   - Be consistent with the accountability campaign.
   - Explain that without accountability, no culture can survive.

4. **Prepare for drama-rama!**
   - Coach junior managers on the difference between gossip and employee problems that merit attention and concern.
   - Make it clear to employees that their rights to open communication do not entitle them to take issue with and endlessly petition decisions.

5. **Curb entitlement through centralized control of your caring program.**
   - The program manager tracks all charitable appeals and decisions.
   - Maintain a moderate approach to incentives.
   - If someone gets greedy, provide a nonthreatening reality check.

6. **A good culture program makes allowances for generational diversity.**
   - Be sensitive to age differences when structuring events.
   - Recognize each generation's unique attitude toward work.
   - Make a serious effort to mentor promising Millennials.
   - Put yourself in their shoes and ask yourself, *Why would a rational human being feel this way?*

7. **Grow the senior team slowly, meticulously, and diplomatically.**
   - Explain the benefits of outside talent to long-term employees.
   - Never rush a senior hire, regardless of operational needs.
   - Warn candidates that your hiring process is longer than the norm.
   - Be prepared to lose a few highly qualified candidates.

8. **Terminations reveal a lot about your culture.**
   - Make managers adhere to a deliberate, compassionate process.
   - Don't let them avoid difficult conversations with their people.
   - An open culture is forthright about its termination policy.
   - Total, immediate transparency is required in layoff situations.
   - Employees who are let go with compassion are appreciative and spread the word.

9. **Don't let bad apples harden your heart.**
   - The ideals of the most giving and progressive culture in the world will occasionally be betrayed by ungrateful employees.
   - Mourn and move on.
   - Do the right thing regardless of the outcome.

10. **Be patient with nonbelievers.**
   - Explain the fiscal reality, i.e., culture *is* profit.
   - Solicit ideas to make sure your culture calendar has broad appeal.

11

The Beryl Experience

By Aubri Levens, Miguel Hernandez, and Jason Armour

We treat everyone like family, not just our employees. That means customers and suppliers as well. Jason Armour is our creative director and is largely responsible for the look and feel of everything Beryl, from logos to materials, websites, and displays. He's written, shot, and produced countless videos, many with me acting like an idiot, but all for a good laugh. Aubri is actually my assistant, and as director of executive wrangling, she is not immune to participating and owning the culture just like any employee. Miguel is a software developer at Beryl, a long-standing member of our IT team.

—Paul

When you think of five-star service—the *crème de la crème* performers in any industry—certain perceptions tend to come to mind: mints on your pillows, personal attention from deliberately pleasant people who've made it a point to learn your name, their willingness to go the extra mile to make an impression, and the resultant confidence you feel in the knowledge that anything you might require is one easy phone call away. Often, five-star service boils down to the power of *details*: a simple word that encompasses the vast difference between an average customer interaction and a memorable, first-class experience.

Interactions at Beryl, with clients, vendors, and coworkers, are all about the details that create an unforgettable experience. Because we take details seriously, these "little things" end up having a huge impact. We consistently and strategically work them into the way we do business, and there are formal processes and procedures in place to make sure nothing falls through the cracks.

Clients Are Family, Too

We want clients to feel that they're a part of the family, every bit as much as our coworkers. From the get-go, we reach out to make sure their Beryl experience is one they can't help but remember. During every initial client implementation, we send a "Welcome Wagon" basket full of goodies. When clients travel to our facility, they find a similar assortment of amenities waiting at their hotel. We tend to hear, "Wow! When I got to my room late last night I was exhausted. Then I opened the door and saw the basket you left, and it just made my trip!"

A guest's visit to the Beryl facility is handled almost as if that person were a foreign dignitary. Before he or she arrives, a visitor notice is posted on our intranet and routed to all involved parties to make sure they know their exact role in creating a five-star guest experience. The guest is immediately greeted by the director of first impressions, who presents a bottle of Beryl water, mints, and a badge with the guest's name and title. She will also have programmed a greeting with the guest's name onto an electronic marquee that scrolls through the lobby.

All guests receive a fun, personalized tour by the culture director, which can include a picture-taking session in our photo booth or Segway lessons if the guest has an interest in those options. Upon departure, all guests receive a special bag of things to help make their travel more pleasant. Fun items in the bag include a fortune cookie that lets them know we feel "fortune-ate" because they visited us, a Beryl Bear stuffed animal, and a special edition of our humorous holiday videos from years past. This provides a great snapshot of our culture. After every visit, the host and the members of the senior leadership team each write the guest a handwritten note that we mail immediately.

Visitors consistently comment on how friendly they find our employees. As a result of our emphasis on hospitality, even unscheduled visitors are greeted as warmly and courteously as if we'd been expecting them for weeks. Coworkers welcome all guests as naturally as if they were in their own homes. A lot of this spontaneity is the result of their daily immersion in a laid-back environment that encourages human beings to simply be themselves.

> *There is an energy, a buzz you feel immediately upon walking into our facility, that draws you in. The bright colors, the friendly faces, and the passion our employees have for Beryl radiates throughout, and it's hard not to become attached to the special environment we have. When you walk through the Beryl doors, you feel welcomed.*
>
> *—Aubri*

Coworker Experience

For many years, our break area consisted of two ordinary, medium-sized rooms. One was filled with vending machines, coffee pots, and microwaves, and the other with dining tables. In spite of the fact that we have more than three hundred employees, the break area was never full. When it finally dawned on us that the space was too bland and uncomfortable, we encouraged coworkers to create their own relaxing, lounge-type environment. Quite a few pitched in, so the budget was minimal.

The stark-white walls and ceiling were painted dark purple. A patient-experience advocate who also happens to be an ace seamstress made curtains, and another donated an aquarium. Our creative director designed wall art, and a software engineer leveraged a personal connection to get us a great deal on a pool table–ping-pong table. We also bought a Wii, a shuffleboard table, and a foosball table. Today, thanks in part to a team lead who volunteered to maintain it each week, the lounge offers employees a relaxing, coffee-house setting. It's full all day, and at 3:00 p.m. a group of IT team members can usually be found playing ping-pong and eating ice cream. Bottom line: *everyone* needs and deserves a break in a culture that works as hard as we do.

> *Stepping away from our projects and clearing our minds keeps us from getting tunnel vision. Most of the time, if I'm stuck on an issue, I can figure it out while I'm playing ping-pong. We also bring in competitors from other departments to help build strong work relationships. Playing a little together helps us build camaraderie and work better together. I always think of the James Earl Jones line in the movie* Best of the Best: *"A team is not a team if you don't give a damn about each other."*
>
> —*Miguel*

Our photo booth is another unique "little thing" that has somehow acquired a larger positive role in the worker experience. The booth is free and prints black-and-white photos on a vertical strip, with a space available for internal branding and logos. We use the booth to commemorate seasonal events like Family Day and the Fall Festival, encouraging coworkers and clients alike to pose with a nearby scarf, cowboy hat, or boa. People love taking these mementos home with them. Since we purchased the booth, it's produced thousands of images that are still floating around, reminding people of the fun family spirit of our culture.

Some culture ideas come easily; others seem to take forever. It took us three years to name our conference rooms! We could easily have kept referring to them as "the downstairs conference room" and "the old training room where marketing used to be," but we saw an opportunity to extend the culture in this apparently trivial exercise. A contest asking coworkers to christen the rooms produced a wide range of options, everything from *Lord of the Rings* characters to well-known Texas rivers. Nothing felt right to us until we looked back on our own corporate history and traditions.

Today the main conference room is named "Granada" after our first client, Granada Hills Hospital. Executive meetings take place in the "Columbia" room upstairs, reminding us of the milestone contract with Columbia/HCA Healthcare Corporation that effectively launched us into the big leagues. Other rooms were duly dubbed "Camry" for the car Paul once gave to an employee; "MPB" for the initials of the three founding brothers; and "ERS," the name of our original startup venture. Two somewhat more "in-joke" room names, "Matador" and "Footloose," recall especially popular—and goofy—scenes from old holiday videos.

Create Traditions

Capturing your own unique "inside" traditions will help spark emotion and allow coworkers to better connect with your organization. We discovered that by giving people the autonomy to be themselves, traditions materialized out of nowhere. For example, no one told our account management group to put together a Fourth of July parade; they just got wild hair wigs one year, dressed up, and paraded around the call center floor. That flash of genius (or insanity) was an immediate highlight of the celebration and has become a progressively more elaborate tradition.

Likewise, we decided one year that it would be fun to create a lighthearted logo for an internal "Customer Service Week" celebration. We put the first design on T-shirts for everyone, and these, too, inspired a tradition. Every year now, we roll out a newly designed shirt. No one knows when to expect them; the shirts just show up one day at a Better Beryl Bureau meeting and we start handing them out. The shirts have been framed over the years and have a special place on the wall in our hallway.

Family Day started out as a simple celebration of our twenty-year milestone. It became so popular that we now always try to outdo ourselves—to the point where Paul once asked the culture director if it would be possible to get a roller coaster for the event. Family Day also spun off another T-shirt tradition. Once the theme has been announced, the children of employees are asked to draw pictures based on that theme. After these pictures are hung up along the hallway, coworkers vote on their favorite and the winning picture becomes the T-shirt everyone receives to wear on Family Day. The culture director mails each employee participant a handwritten thank-you note, often with a five-dollar Toys "R" Us gift card for each child who entered. All of the winning drawings have been framed and are on permanent display.

Beryl's version of *The Gong Show* was a simple talent show. But we thought it would be fun to encourage "bad" acts as well. This has become an annual event since 2003. All staff is invited to participate or watch the day-long event. We have a stage, spotlights, and judges, too. Our leadership team enjoys impersonating their favorite reality-show judge and they don't hesitate to "gong" a bad act. It provides a day of laughs and energy for the entire company and serves as a showcase for some unknown talents among the staff.

We hang virtually *all* of our history and memories on the walls, some of which have been specifically dedicated to different aspects of the culture. One is covered with photos of historical events and parties; another—the "Beryl Bear Wall"—is covered with vacation pictures of coworkers holding our little stuffed mascot. The Beryl Bear has been to Times Square, the White House, Disneyland, the Eiffel Tower, and numerous European castles. In the course of many mountain-climbing expeditions and ocean cruises, he's also become our in-house equivalent of the "Flat Stanley" phenomenon and a great way for coworkers to bond in a fun, creative, and cooperative endeavor. Employees frequently tell us they're careful to make sure they have the bear with them before they leave on vacation so they and their families can provide—and proudly be seen in—the next picture on the wall.

> *One of my favorite maxims is, "If there isn't a picture of it, it didn't happen." We all forget things, so it's nice to go down the hall, glance over, and see a picture of yourself sliding down a slide with a favorite coworker. We love to remind everyone of the fun and camaraderie we have.*
>
> —*Jason*

Paul and his brother Barry were unable to attend the company's 2001 holiday party, so they made a short, simple video with a few jokes in it to wish everyone a happy holiday. Employees loved it and the creative director decided to make one in 2002. Over the years, these videos have kept getting funnier and more ingenious, and the project has morphed into a major extravaganza that people really look forward to for months before the party. The creative director writes a clever script and shoots the video, giving roles to different employees. Paul is always costumed as the main character, and has starred in dead-on spoofs of blockbusters like *Footloose*, *Forrest Gump*, and *The Hangover*. One year he performed a musical version of a Beryl tour. People are thrilled when we ask them to be in the video or help with production.

One of our team leads thought a bowling league would be a great idea. He drummed up interest, coordinated payroll deductions, and designed cool bowling shirts. Now Friday nights are major events with a large contingent invading a local bowling alley for camaraderie and competition. Many employees who don't bowl come along just to hang out with their peers.

What can you say about something as mundane as a corporate dress code policy? Well, a lot of folks say our dress code rocks! We were originally a business-casual environment, but as the years went by we grew more and more casual. Minimal guidelines keep employees from looking like they just rolled out of bed, and we trust them to choose their own attire even when important client prospects are scheduled to visit. We're proud of our culture and who we are, and people take the privilege seriously because nobody wants to lose it.

During the entire month of December—and this is where our culture really makes some old-school types cringe—it's perfectly fine to wear sweats or pajamas to work. How this tradition got started no one can precisely recall, but everyone agrees that "sweats and pajamas month" is tremendously enjoyable. The underlying message is: "Whew! We just wrapped up another profitable and productive year, so let's do a little therapeutic relaxing before we have to knuckle down again in January!"

Can you list the traditions in your organization? If not, powerful ones can easily begin to take shape if you allow employees to run with their own fun ideas.

More Little Things

There are so many other little things that make coming to work here more of an experience than just an average job. If someone doesn't feel well, we offer a service that sends a nurse practitioner within the hour to work or home to deliver medicine, soup, and prescriptions. This is much appreciated by a person who may know he has a simple sinus infection and doesn't want to waste a whole day waiting to see a doctor. If coworkers work out at least ten times a month, we reimburse their monthly fitness club dues. We reimburse for Weight Watchers meetings, too, if the participant keeps a food log and shows success. Every department has their own Keurig coffee machine with company-supplied coffee cartridges. We also maintain an intranet site called "Beryl Bargains," where employees can post personal items they want to sell.

Recognition campaigns? Most serious businesses take a halfhearted stab at this. They'll have a roster of employees who get a standard card on their anniversaries saying, "Thanks for staying with the company for five years." It's a nice gesture, but you couldn't blame anyone for being underwhelmed. Paul takes recognition a step further by sending a personal card to each employee's home. These spontaneous, event-related cards extend the connections made by the personal anniversary cards mentioned in chapter 6. It's all part of our Beryl Cares outreach program.

Our culture director pays close attention to what's happening in employees' lives, and she keeps us posted throughout the year so that Paul and Lance can make timely personal connections. If a coworker becomes a grandmother, the culture director sends her an e-mail and the group extends congratulations with a personal note. If somebody tears their ACL on a ski trip, that person will get a handwritten card the same week saying something like, "Sorry to hear about the accident and hope the knee's getting better!" or whatever the guys want to say. There's no norm and no formality about it, and that's the whole point. On a day-to-day basis, the executives may have little to no interaction with the recipient, but they want to make sure he or she knows that management cares. On these cards, the sender always writes something that relates *specifically* to each individual.

The Big Picture

Let's face it: no business is going to thrive, much less redefine its industry, just because they send their prospects gift baskets or because they put a pool table in the break room. Life isn't that easy. Beryl's obsession with operational details no matter how little they may seem does, however, have a bottom-line impact that helps explain our success.

An important thing to keep in mind: no matter how manic we get about perfect execution, micromanagement is a big no-no here. Nobody is looking over your shoulder with a checklist to make sure you cross every *t* and dot every *i*. In fact, employees are encouraged to take the initiative themselves to identify and implement the different details that eventually make a process perfect. If you can make things more efficient for clients, by all means use your autonomy to do so! Employees know that we welcome fresh ideas, and there are numerous intranet forums available for these. If the suggestions are culture-related, post them in the "Ask Lara" section. If they have to do with the call center operations, air them out on "Ask Lindy." If you want the CEO's attention, there's always "Ask Paul."

The Magic Word

Ultimately, the most important part of any culture is *consistency*, a virtue that we emphasize 24–7. Think about your favorite restaurant, a place where you've probably come to expect a certain quality of food and service. When those expectations aren't met, you leave disappointed—more so than you might have been if you'd never been wowed there in the first place.

When our coworkers depend on something and it doesn't happen, that, too, can create disappointment—even resentment— inside our shop. For instance, when internal interviews are conducted for a position, the hiring manager is normally required to complete a feedback form for every applicant. The manager must also review this form with every applicant before we make an offer to the successful candidate. We dropped the ball once in a big way when a coworker got zero official feedback on her interview and then learned through the grapevine that someone else got the job. She was so upset that she left us for another company. Seriously, who can blame her? If the hiring manager had been *consistent*—if he had provided the timely feedback that the applicant had every reason to expect—she would almost certainly still be working here today.

A major key to Beryl's success has been our ability to drive consistency down to the detail level. Consistency is the magic word when it comes to customer service, both internally and externally. That's why we insist that *every* received communication—e-mails, voice mails, suggestion box submissions—*must* be answered in twenty-four hours. Rules like that are demanding on busy days, but they help guarantee that every person we touch gets the best possible Beryl experience.

Five stars all the way, every single time!

Tips and Tools

1. **Clients are family, too.**
   - Make your clients feel welcome by involving them in your culture.
   - All the little details can make a big impact.
   - Don't be afraid to have fun with your clients.
   - A simple, personal, handwritten thank-you note will make your client feel special and connected.

2. **Emphasize a positive coworker experience.**
   - Create a space where coworkers will want to decompress, recharge, and connect with one another during the workday.
   - Involve coworkers with the creation, decoration, and utilization of your facility. Let them make it their own in small ways.

3. **Create traditions.**
   - Capturing your own unique "inside" traditions will help spark emotion and allow coworkers to better connect with your organization.
   - Commemorate your traditions with T-shirts, crazy photos—anything that keeps them alive.
   - Dress-up days and a relaxed dress code are ways to celebrate while still being cost-effective.

4. **Utilize more "little things."**
   - Become a part of your coworkers' everyday lives by offering reimbursement programs and celebrating in their successes and life events.
   - Reach out personally to coworkers through note cards.

5. Always keep the big picture in sight.
   - Allow coworkers to take initiative and accountability for their work.
   - Encourage autonomy.

6. Remember the magic word.
   - Implement a culture of consistency.

Afterword

There are clear choices in the way that business is conducted, and I think the cultural model presented in this book is the best way. We choose to put people first, and we choose to be a premium provider, knowing that there will be an impact on our success. If there wasn't a clear correlation between an ethical, empowered workforce and profitable operations, I certainly would have had much more difficulty sustaining Beryl for the last twenty-six years.

My hope is that models like this become much more common. To advance that goal, I recently helped form a community of like-minded business owners with Bo Burlingham, the author of the internationally published *Small Giants: Companies That Choose to Be Great Instead of Big*. The Small Giants Community (www.smallgiants. org), now operative in more than twelve countries, is comprised of successful small- and medium-sized private companies with a common desire to be special because of who they are, not how big they can get. The focus is not so much on business plans and financials as on the behaviors that allow us to become intimate with our employees, our stakeholders, and our community in a nontraditional sense. As the book you've just read indicates, it's all about being values-driven and building evolved cultures that make the world a better place.

Sometimes a company has to make hard choices to live up to these ideals. Beryl recently let go of its largest client, one of the few nonhospital operations we serve. This company had grown quite large over the years, but their approach to business changed and they wanted us to change with them. When they tried to take us in a direction we weren't comfortable with from an ethical perspective, we made the decision to part ways. That decision had a big impact on our revenue, and the entire senior leadership team—myself included—was more than a little worried about the challenge moving forward.

But the reaction of the company to the news amazed us all, and reminded us that even in a tough economy, our company stands for something different. Here's an example:

From: Quintana, Carmen
Sent: Wednesday, August 19, 2009 11:57 PM
To: Spiegelman, Paul
Subject: RE: Business Update

Hi Paul,
Greg and Maricela informed our team about [the former client] earlier today. I understand the large impact this will have on Beryl's yearly revenue, but I have to honestly say that I was glad to hear the news.

Since [the former client] started using telemarketing firm(s) to bring in sales, I felt that there were dishonest practices being used based on the many caller complaints about unauthorized credit card charges. I spoke with several frustrated and some panicked callers who all repeated the same story . . . they declined the [client] program along with other offerings, but were still charged for them. This was a hardship for the elderly callers who were on fixed incomes. It was beginning to feel like I was part of a "scam" and my conscience began to bother me. It wasn't the Beryl Way.

If [the former client] keeps using these same practices, they'll acquire a negative reputation and that will become their "brand" and eventually their undoing. Smart consumers like to research products and they'll read the product or company reviews on the Internet before making a purchase. Therefore, if Beryl continued the relationship with [the former client], they would be associated with the negative brand and their reputation would be tarnished because of it.

Thanks for the update and for not compromising our values and brand.

—Carmen Q

After I read that e-mail and dozens more like it, my reaction was basically, "Wow! We just lost our biggest customer—and I couldn't be happier!" Because when you have a loyal group of people who believe in your vision, money no longer has to be your primary concern. You've evolved the culture of your organization to the point where people power will carry you through almost any economic setback.

Real business leaders may also have to make *personal* sacrifices to protect their culture and the people who are important to them. Not long ago, I was looking to diversify my duties in a way that would free me up a bit to focus more on the Small Giants Community and The Beryl Institute (our thought leadership–research entity). I also wanted to help our leadership team take advantage of the growing opportunity for our business in the healthcare market. A private equity firm made a great offer for the company: more money than I could spend, plenty of resources to invest in the business going forward, and a group of people I thought I could work with. Very importantly, the firm was willing to take a long-term approach to the deal and promised to honor our people-centric philosophy.

Shortly after signing a letter of intent, I started to have serious misgivings. As much as this private equity team appreciated the idea of a progressive culture, their passion was numbers. I realized that by definition, they existed to build shareholder value for their investors. There is nothing wrong with that, but that's not the business we're in. We're in a values-based business that makes the world a better place. We exist primarily to enhance the lives of the people that work here. I started to feel a much shorter-term type of pressure that I'd never felt before. Ultimately, I walked away from the deal at the eleventh hour because I just don't think that what we have and what we want going forward is compatible with the type of firm where numbers come first.

Why did I suddenly feel such a huge weight lifting off my shoulders as I waved good-bye to my own big payday? Was it because I've met so many former CEOs who had cashed out of their companies and waved good-bye to their people without a second thought? Some of those talented, analytical guys will tell me now how they're roaming the planet, climbing mountains and looking for the real meaning of life. Why do I always get a sense that the answer was staring them in the face for years before they took the money and walked away?

In retrospect, I almost gave in to the same temptation by letting the dollar signs outweigh my ultimate goal. And subconsciously, I was probably hoping I could have it both ways. Maybe, on top of the personal profit, I could expand a business and still preserve the values-based culture. Maybe, just maybe, I could take all that good vibration stuff into a deal with new partners who basically buy low and sell high for a living and still maintain my integrity. It seemed like a fascinating challenge at the time, but right now I'd have to say that it looks like a really difficult equation to master.

When a business leader seriously reflects on his or her life and legacy, immediate family will naturally be the first concern. But after that, I don't think my judge and jury will be friends, fellow

CEOs, or professional organizations. Any serious business leader's ultimate judge and jury will be the employees he or she empowers. On a practical level, the grateful messages I continue to receive from the members of my Beryl family are a concrete testimony to the power and value of an evolved culture program. On a personal level, honestly, they're worth more than anything money can buy.

The ultimate lesson is a simple one: if you're fortunate enough in life to find something that really makes you happy, stick with it! Because ultimately, even a bottom-up culture can't help reflecting the spirit of its leaders. If those owners and managers are passionately pursuing what truly makes them happy, the whole business will respond to that spirit. This book is a road map, and hopefully some of the lessons will help you get where you want to go on your life's journey. At the end of the road, don't be surprised if you look back and see that you've shown quite a few smiling people the way.

—Paul Spiegelman

About the Contributors

Name: Jason Armour

Title: Creative Director

Job Description: I generally handle creative for the four Beryl companies as well as champion quirky culture things, like the photo booth or our Traveling Bear wall. Any given day I'm wearing a number of different hats—I may be hard-coding to build an interactive website, taking photos of a golf tournament, filming our CEO acting like a fool, or performing more serious marketing efforts.

I was honored and excited about being able to share some stories from my time here that may inspire other businesses to improve their workplace cultures. Every other company I worked for had some "corporate office" in another state that was making decisions that affected our lives. There would be some policy that didn't make sense being enforced by an absent presence. At Beryl, *we* are the headquarters. If something doesn't make sense, we change it. Also, when the "owners" at other companies came to visit, we'd all have to clean our desks, no personal items, dress up nice, etc. It was intimidating. Paul puts on a bear costume.

Name: Melissa Barnes

Title: Director of Patient Experience Team and Strategic Account Executive

Job Description: I work with the client-facing team and customers to impact and measure employee experience, patient experience, and various healthcare initiatives.

Beryl has a "family"-style approach with genuine compassion for team members. Every one of us truly understands the ultimate purpose: helping patients receive the care, information, and tools they need to feel better and be in better health. But also, I truly appreciate the team I work with, the customers we partner with, and the real impact of what we do. Just as with our callers, we want our team members to receive the care, information, and tools they need to feel better and be better.

Name: Melissa Bloom

Title: Strategic Account Executive

Job Description: I have the privilege of working closely with one of Beryl's top clients. My primary responsibilities include managing and growing the relationship.

My first meeting at Beryl was a business review led by Paul. Our management team was collectively discussing the pros and cons of keeping a particular Beryl client. I have been in management and sales for my entire adult career and I had never before experienced anything like that meeting. Paul genuinely cared about how others were treated and our continued challenges with that client, and he involved the whole team in reviewing the state of the relationship. It blew me away. There continue to be other examples of leadership, but that first experience stayed with me. We don't have the best equipment, furniture, computers, or facility. The people make it special. I have been overwhelmed by the willingness of others to pitch in, do the right thing, solve an issue, and connect with me on the deepest level. Amazing people.

Name: Lindy Butterfield
Title: Vice President of Operations
Job Description: I lead the best team in the organization! We are responsible for communicating with patients every day via phone, e-mail, and chat on behalf of our clients. We refer patients to physicians, register people for classes and health seminars, schedule appointments, and provide discharge services, which helps patients returning home understand their discharge instructions. I have the privilege to work with a management team that focuses on coaching and development of their team members, while ensuring the business runs proficiently and productively. Finally, I oversee the support team—including the quality department, performance support specialists, and the workforce management team. They are here to support the advocates and management team, as well as the rest of the organization, to deliver a quality and timely experience at each encounter.

I love working for a company that has given me the autonomy to develop a strong management team and implement more efficiency and quality measures within the department, all while being creative and enhancing the culture. I have the best work–life balance that I have ever had in my career. Beryl *rocks!*

Name: Tina Clay

Title: Data Specialist

Job Description: I am responsible for transcribing physician, class, and service data into databases and coordinating daily support activities for designated clients. I provide support to both clients and account managers for daily account management activities. I also work with clients to ensure that information is accurate and adequate for executing their marketing initiatives.

Beryl has instilled my commitment to accountability. I must be accountable for all that I do in every area. I have been encouraged to reach out to others. I smile all the time. I greet every person I encounter with a smile and a "how ya doing?" It's taught me that it's not always what I do or say, but how. Our core values are implemented at home as well. My husband knows each of the values just from reading our *Beryl Life* magazine. When I have my "down" days, he reminds me of those values and encourages me to look at situations with a new set of eyes.

Name: Glenda Dearion

Title: Talent Manager

Job Description: I am responsible for managing our recruiting team as well as delivering all facets (internal and external) of the recruiting success throughout the organization.

I felt honored to know Beryl wanted my voice to be heard. Anyone who knows me understands how important loyalty and family are to me. Beryl is truly a place I can call my home away from home and my second family. Beryl has proven how important it considers my health and well-being. Even with a busy schedule or a crazy work week (or month), Beryl demands I take time to enjoy myself and my family. I am thankful to be a family member of Beryl!

Name: Patrick Gonzales

Title: Patient-Experience Advocate—Marketing Services

Job Description: I help people find physicians and classes in their community.

I think what sets Beryl apart is the family feeling that you get from your coworkers. It doesn't matter if you work on the phones or IT or management—you get the sense that they really care about you. I had barely finished training when I became sick and had to spend two weeks in the hospital. To my surprise, I received a get-well card from Paul. It really made an impression on me that Beryl was a company that cared.

Name: Miguel Hernandez

Title: Lead Senior Software Engineer

Job Description: I develop new and innovative software solutions that will connect people to healthcare.

I've been working for Beryl for nine years and it's been a great experience. I've seen the company grow so much that I don't know half the people working here! Hiring new employees and increasing profit in a down economy does say a lot about the company. Being the premier premium provider and a nine-time "Best Places to Work" award winner makes me feel that I made a great decision in working for Beryl. I work with a great team and they are the reason I stay and work hard in helping the company achieve its goals. Beryl has given me the opportunity to provide my family with a better home, better activities, and, most of all, family time. Seeing the smiles on my kids' faces makes the thousands of lines of code I've written throughout the years well worth it.

Name: Jhan Knebel

Title: Senior Instructional Systems Designer

Job Description: I am responsible for analyzing training needs and identifying solutions. I then develop and deliver those solutions to the organization and our clients. I also mentor others in the area of instructional design.

I love working at a company that really focuses on improving the lives of all with whom we interact. From the commitment to educating coworkers to each and every patient we speak with, we make a difference every day in people's lives!

Name: Nancy Lecroy

Title: Vice President of Marketing

Job Description: I am responsible for the development and implementation of marketing and communications strategies with the aim of growing the business and enhancing Beryl's brand and awareness.

As marketers and brand managers, we're always looking for that diamond in the rough—that one thing we can promote that will set the organization apart from the competition. At Beryl, I had the opposite challenge. I had so many to choose from: service, product innovation, industry leader (just to name a few). But the one thing that rose to the top was the people. A brand is only as good as the person delivering it to the customer, and my coworkers at Beryl take that job very seriously. They live by the brand principles and use them to guide their actions throughout the day. They take pride in delivering on our brand promise and recognize the important role each person plays in bringing the brand to life. At Beryl, we say to each other, "You are the face of Beryl." And it's true!

Name: Aubri Levens

Title: Director of Executive Wrangling

Job Description: Essentially, I am the executive assistant to our glorious founder and CEO, Paul Spiegelman. My responsibility is to keep Paul on the right track and organized on a daily basis.

I love to come to work, I love my coworkers, and I believe in Beryl. That's the difference to me—like night and day from where I came from. I feel more engaged in my life now . . . I am able to enjoy my time with my family and not stress about work. There is no price on the freedom that Beryl has provided me.

One final thought: the people and views in this book are genuine. We are not doing this to sell books, get famous, or make money; we wrote these words because we love this company and the people that make it great every day.

Name: Jennifer Limon

Title: Human Resources Manager

Job Description: I am responsible for managing our benefit and compensation programs. I strive to ensure that Beryl offers a great benefits package that is cost-efficient for everyone.

I have worked at Beryl for ten years. I am very blessed to say that I still look forward to coming to work each day. Being in the position that I'm in, I get to see a lot of things. We are not perfect by any means, but I truly feel in my heart that we care about our employees and have a strong focus on maintaining our core values in all that we do. I completely stand behind this company and what we stand for.

Name: Elaine McCullough
Title: Patient-Experience Advocate—RedBrick Health
Job Description: I work with employees of Fortune 500 companies to take charge of their health through proactive and consultative telephone and e-mail lifestyle management support.

Being asked to participate in Paul's book was such a wonderful honor, and in fact, it was very interesting to be part of its development. There are two key things about Beryl that have affected my work life as well as my personal life: we help people, and we make a difference in lives. Beryl also values the people within its own four walls and allows us the creativity to shine.

Name: Jennifer McDonald
Title: Instructional Designer and Trainer (a.k.a. Instructional Activities Artist)
Job Description: I am responsible for creating and training new and existing curriculum based on business needs. I have been privileged to be involved in everything from team building for support staff to new-hire training for our advocates.

Beryl is like no other place I have ever worked. I feel truly blessed to come to work every day and work with my Beryl family. People here believe in each other and visibly uphold the Beryl values every day. We work hard but we play hard. The people are what make Beryl great!

Name: Jennifer Mills

Title: Data Specialist and Member Management Administrator for both The Beryl Institute and Small Giants Community

Job Description: I am responsible for member relations for The Beryl Institute and the Small Giants Community, serving as the first touch point for member and guest inquiries. I manage all day-to-day operations and member information, and I serve as a resource in ensuring an unparalleled experience.

I am in a unique position of being able to work for multiple entities under the Beryl umbrella. My commitment to Beryl's culture and team camaraderie has guided my growth at Beryl. Right before I started working at Beryl, I moved thousands of miles away from my family. Finding Beryl has become one of the biggest blessings of my life. Beryl is my family! I am extremely honored to contribute to the *Smile Guide*!

Name: Lara Morrow

Title: Queen of Fun and Laughter

Job Description: I manage all programs and activities around the culture in the organization: events, parties, community outreach, onboarding, recognition and morale, internal communications, and the program that helps employees through personal struggles or celebrations.

There could never be another job like the one I have at Beryl. I have a front-row seat to see how Beryl impacts others' lives. It doesn't get much better than that. When an employee is going through a crisis, part of my job is to jump in and help him or her through it. Most companies say things like, "Don't bring your problems to work!" At Beryl, we want our employees to know that we are here to support them. Our loyalty toward them results in their undying loyalty to the company.

Name: Andrew Pryor
Title: Vice President of the Department of Great People and Fun
Job Description: I am responsible for the recruitment, development, and retention of our outstanding performers and world-class talent.

The main difference at Beryl is that I am empowered to care for our coworkers on a personal basis—to respect them as individuals and look at each coworker's unique set of circumstances and career aspirations. Beryl's culture reminds me every day that in my role as a leader, I am empowered to help others, enable career opportunities, encourage talent to take a chance on a new role, and guide young or inexperienced coworkers toward their career goals. I see my role as a leader at Beryl as an opportunity to impact the lives and careers of our coworkers.

Name: Rochelle Revel
Title: Patient-Experience Advocate—Post-Discharge Services
Job Description: I call patients recently discharged from the hospital to find out how they are doing now that they are home, and what kind of care they received at the hospital. My call is either the last or one of the last contacts the hospital will have with the patient, so the patient experience on that call is very important.

The biggest difference at Beryl is the attitude of your fellow employees. Most everyone here looks forward to coming to work every day, and that affects the outlook of the day, conversations between employees, and the work attitude. Being around happy people helps me want to do my job better.

I felt completely honored to participate in the writing of the book. At my last job, they didn't care what I thought. I really can't thank Paul enough for all he does to make sure that I have a happy, safe, encouraging place to work. Thanks, Paul!

Name: Sandy Reyna
Title: Data Analyst
Job Description: I work on various projects that require pulling data from different resources, analyzing it, and putting it into a format that can be useful for the client or for management to make decisions.

Working at Beryl is different from other places because of the value it places on the employee. There is a true sense of family, and when one member is hurting we rally around for support. Because of this, employees are passionate about doing their job to ensure Beryl is successful.

Name: LaToya Robinson
Title: Senior Data Specialist
Job Description: I am responsible for assisting my team lead with managing the day-to-day operations of the data specialist team.

I have been able to grow and learn how to build long-lasting relationships. My family looks forward to helping out in the community. And I believe Beryl's culture has allowed me to motivate and encourage others in a caring way. Beryl realized that I love to see others smile and that I have a personal connection with my peers.

I know that I am not Beryl's perfect employee, but when I was asked to be a part of this book, I finally realized that Beryl values me as a person. I am not just a number or just an employee. This company truly cares about my well-being, and for that I am humbled and blessed.

Name: Maricela Rodriguez
Title: Director of Operations
Job Description: I manage the business. I am responsible for ensuring there is staff available to answer incoming calls from customers across the country. I coach, counsel, and motivate managers to meet or exceed our business metrics. I also partner with internal customers to ensure we are meeting our clients' expectations daily.

At Beryl, we value our employees, we value our customers, and we celebrate success. It's a very simplified point of view, but it's what we do!

Name: Lance Shipp
Title: Chief Operating Officer
Job Description: I oversee all the day-to-day operations of Beryl—and fill in for Paul quite a bit.

I tell every new class of coworkers this observation: "If your personal values align with Beryl's five core values, then you have found a home." I have worked for companies both large and small, good and bad, but it is energizing to come to work every day knowing you can help people grow, succeed, and be an instrument of change. I am proud that readers will get to hear the voices of so many of the coworkers who make Beryl a special place.

Name: Bob Willey

Title: Leadership Development Consultant

Job Description: I am responsible for ensuring that all support staff employees at Beryl receive the necessary learning opportunities to maximize performance. I am also responsible for developing and maintaining a leadership platform based on core competencies for success.

I am proud to be associated with one of the most forward-thinking companies in America. Beryl's commitment to excellence is evident in every department and the actions and attitudes of everyone who works here.

Name: Greg Williams

Title: Operations Manager

Job Description: My coworkers and I are responsible for all operational aspects of client relationships, through ongoing communications with account contacts (internally and externally) and promoting customer goodwill, loyalty, and confidence. This includes the coordination of department responses, managing teams to client-specific requirements by demonstrating a genuine concern for the quality of work performed for the client, and assisting in the nurturing of team members. I also provide development for the team leads to ensure they are able to support business goals. My team and I strive to provide exceptional patient experience to make each of our clients a client for life!

Beryl is the first company I've worked for where the pyramid is adamantly managed from the bottom up. Generally, the focus is on an individual basis; at Beryl, however, each and every one of the employees *matters*. The way my coworkers spring into action to help each other is mind-boggling. We all have our own personal struggles, but that's all out the window in a moment's notice when one of our own is in need. It is this type of commitment to each other, our clients, and the organization that makes me proud to be the face of Beryl!

About Paul

Paul Spiegelman is the founder and chief executive officer of The Beryl Companies, which includes: Beryl, a technology-focused patient-experience company dedicated to improving relationships between healthcare providers and consumers; The Beryl Institute, a research and educational entity that publishes information about improving the patient experience and how that activity links to better financial outcomes for healthcare providers; The Circle, a training company that helps businesses enhance employee engagement and develop more positive workplace cultures; and the Small Giants Community, a global organization that brings together leaders who are focused on values-based business principles.

Paul leads a unique, people-centric culture that has remarkably high employee and customer retention rates. Beryl has won nine "best place to work" awards, including being voted the No. 2 Best Medium-Sized Company to Work for in America. Paul was named regional Entrepreneur of the Year 2010 by Ernst & Young.

Paul is a sought-after speaker and author on executive leadership, entrepreneurship, corporate culture, customer relationships, and employee engagement. His views have been published in the *New York Times*, *Entrepreneur*, the *Dallas Morning News*, *Inc. Magazine*,

Healthcare Financial Management, Leadership Excellence, and many other noteworthy publications, as well as in his first internationally published book, *Why is Everyone Smiling? The Secret Behind Passion, Productivity, and Profit.*

Paul practiced law for two years prior to starting Beryl. He holds a bachelor's degree in history from the University of California Los Angeles and a law degree from Southwestern University in Los Angeles. He mentors MBA students at Texas Christian University and Southern Methodist University, as well as nurse executives in the Robert Wood Johnson Executive Nurse Fellows Program. He is a member of the American College of Healthcare Executives and on the board of the nonprofit Entrepreneurs for North Texas.